CATHOLIC PARISHES OF THE 21ST CENTURY

CATHOLIC PARISHES OF THE 21ST CENTURY

CHARLES E. ZECH,
MARY L. GAUTIER,
MARK M. GRAY,
JONATHON L. WIGGINS,
AND
THOMAS P. GAUNT, S.J.

OXFORD
UNIVERSITY PRESS

OXFORD
UNIVERSITY PRESS

Oxford University Press is a department of the University of Oxford. It furthers the University's objective of excellence in research, scholarship, and education by publishing worldwide. Oxford is a registered trade mark of Oxford University Press in the UK and certain other countries.

Published in the United States of America by Oxford University Press
198 Madison Avenue, New York, NY 10016, United States of America.

CIP data is on file at the Library of Congress

ISBN 978–0–19–064516–8

1 3 5 7 9 8 6 4 2

Printed by Sheridan Books, Inc., United States of America

CONTENTS

FOREWORD

"The Spirit is leading us into an unanticipated future." These are the words I often use to describe the remarkable findings of the Emerging Models of Pastoral Leadership Project. Begun in 2003, this project, part of the Lilly Endowment's Sustaining Pastoral Excellence Program, was designed to identify and promote emerging pastoral leadership models that sustain vibrant Catholic parish communities. With the advent of the project a new era of parish research began, allowing us to witness the increasingly challenging leadership demands and structural issues of the Catholic parish in the United States.

Thanks to the vision of the National Association for Lay Ministry, which undertook the Emerging Models Project, working in partnership with the Conference for Pastoral Planning and Council Development, the National Catholic Young Adult Ministry Conference, the National Association of Catholic Personnel Administrators, the National Association of Diaconate Directors, and the National Federation of Priests' Councils, and with the generosity of the Lilly Endowment, we had the ability to look at these issues. Over the next six years the project would work with pastoral leaders, theologians, canon lawyers, and researchers to study and understand the parish of today. Separate studies with differing modalities were conducted in pastoral leadership, lay ministry, young adults in ministry, the use of canon 517.2 (parish life coordinators), and multiple-parish ministry.

When, as the first director of the Emerging Models Project, I spoke of the changing paradigms of the parish, I would begin by referring to the old movie *The Bells of St. Mary's* to remind people of the parish prior to Vatican II. In that movie the associate pastor, played by a young, blue-eyed Bing Crosby, showed kindness to the elderly pastor, women religious teachers, parishioners, and children alike. Today most people have never even heard of the movie, much less remember a parish like that. Those who do will recall that the Church world seemed quite stable in the 1950s. Parishes were growing; pastors and associate pastors were the sole providers of ministry. There was no parish staff other than a housekeeper and maintenance personnel. The school—and there usually was one attached to the parish—was run by an order of sisters who taught large numbers of students for minimal compensation. Then along came Vatican II with its *aggiornamento*, (a bringing up to date) which did indeed open windows and let fresh air into the Church. Parishes began integrating the developments of the Council, and new life was happening everywhere.

In this climate a wonderful opportunity came up for a nationwide study of U.S. parishes. Published in 1989, the Notre Dame Study of Catholic Parish Life, surveyed 1,039 parishes, offering the largest and most significant research of its kind. The key finding of this study was, yes, *change*. The Notre Dame researchers offered the U.S. Church a significant snapshot of Catholic parish life, and it was a very different picture from the parish of the 1950s. While some of the study's findings were not surprising, parish life in the late 20th century had certainly changed. Dioceses were seeing the migration of parishioners from city to suburb and the exodus of young people from rural areas. The majority of Catholics still lived in the U.S. heartland, even as waves of immigration were just beginning to change the familiar European multiculturalism to a multiculturalism of global origins. Every parish had its own pastor, and parishioners were volunteering in liturgical and catechetical ministries. Laity began providing consultation on parish pastoral and finance councils. The first lay ministers joined parish staffs, primarily women religious who were moving from school teaching to pastoral ministry. Lay people taught in Catholic schools, and permanent deacons were being ordained. And although the U.S. Church still saw itself as growing, declines in schools and vocations to the priesthood and religious life were starting to appear.

As Emerging Models researchers studied pastoral leadership in today's Church, they quickly found that the model of parish life described by the Notre Dame Study was in many ways becoming obsolete. We are living into the next wave of change in every part of the United States as dioceses are working to provide parish life adapted to the changing resources and demographics available to them. The old adage "Necessity is the mother of invention' is taking on a whole new meaning, and multiple paradigms of parish life and ministry are coming into play. Today's pastoral leaders and parishioners are being asked to reimagine who does ministry, what leadership looks like, and where and what a parish is.

To better understand these changes, the Emerging Models Project commissioned the Center for Applied Research in the Apostolate (CARA) to conduct a study of U.S. parishes and pastoral leaders. I remember the growing excitement in our initial meetings as representatives of the Emerging Models Project and CARA researchers realized we had the opportunity to create a trend study that would expand the work of the original Notre Dame researchers. With today's technology and the generosity of the Lilly Endowment, the research moved forward, engaging the questions asked in the 1989 study along with additional questions required by the Church reality of today.

So, beginning in 2009, CARA conducted a study based on a partially stratified random sample of 5,549 U.S. parishes, roughly three times the size of the Notre Dame study. The respondents finally interviewed for the study were from 3,500 parishes chosen in such a way as to ensure a full and accurate representation of parishes across the nation. The study consisted of a series of three surveys, the first of which was a single-informant survey sent to parishes to develop a portrait of parish life in the United States today. This was followed by a survey of parish leaders in a subsample of 60 of these parishes and in-pew surveys with their parishioners. The results were stunning.

Contained in this volume are the results of the Emerging Models Project conducted by CARA. The interpretation and application of these findings are left to the reader. Do know that what you will find is *change*. It is critically important that bishops, pastors, planners, parish staff, and parishioners all begin to grasp what is upon us. The Church of the 1980s still holds a nostalgic place in our religious imagination and shows up in discussions about how to move forward. But if we hope to maintain parish vitality in today's world, we must study these emerging trends and prepare for a different future. We can all be very grateful to CARA for providing us with a look at today's parish world. Please spend time with what you find here. Live with it. Share it with councils, staff, and committees. Find ways to animate "total ministering communities" of missionary disciples in which all are co-responsible for entering into Jesus's mission of bringing about the kingdom of God. We wish you well as you move into this unanticipated future.

Marti R. Jewell, D.Min.,
associate professor, University of Dallas,
School of Ministry, director emeritus of
the Emerging Models of Pastoral
Leadership Project
2015

CATHOLIC PARISHES OF THE 21ST CENTURY

CHAPTER ONE

INTRODUCTION

In the structure of the Catholic Church the local parish is where members experience religion firsthand. It is there they worship, are educated in the faith, receive their sacraments, and form community. All parishes are complex social organizations, combining varying elements of leadership, finances, worship styles, community outreach programs, and approaches to religious education, and are populated by diverse generational cohorts and ethnic groups, each with their own concerns and traditions. Nevertheless they are all members of the universal Church. While all parishes share some underlying commonalities, all are different. It is vitally important that Church leaders understand local parish activities.

It is not surprising that Catholic parish life has been the focus of a significant amount of social science research. Noted scholars such as Fr. Joseph Fichter SJ, Fr. Philip J. Murnion, William D'Antonio, Dean Hoge, James Davidson, and Fr. Eugene Hemrick have employed state-of-the-art survey research techniques to analyze a variety of Catholic parish topics. The researchers at the Center for Applied Research in the Apostolate have been providing valuable research for over 50 years, but a seminal moment in the study of U.S. Catholic parish life came with the publication in the 1980s of a series of reports from the groundbreaking Notre Dame Study of Catholic Parish Life.

THE NOTRE DAME STUDY OF CATHOLIC PARISH LIFE

Focusing on U.S. parish life twenty years after the Second Vatican Council, the Notre Dame Study was an interdisciplinary effort to understand parish life in the 1980s. Phase 1 was based on survey responses received from key informants (typically the pastor) from 1,099 parishes. This was followed by Phase 2, which took an in-depth look at 36 parishes that had completed the Phase 1 survey. Phase 2 conducted individual surveys of pastors, paid staff, volunteer leaders, and parishioners; each parish was visited by field staff who conducted interviews and made observations of parish life. The study concluded with Phase 3, which interpreted and applied the findings.

Outcomes of the Notre Dame Study included fifteen separate reports, four books, more than a dozen journal articles, and a handful of dissertations, covering nearly every aspect of parish life. Among its primary findings were the following:

- The changing roles of parish leadership, with lay parishioners increasingly involved in parish decision making.
- Changes in parishioners' devotional lives, especially in the many ways Mass is celebrated along with a dramatic decrease in weekly Mass attendance; clear generational differences in church devotions.
- A decline in parochial schools combined with an emphasis on religious education taught by lay parishioners.
- Increasing multiculturalism primarily due to the growth in the number of Hispanic parishioners.
- The migration of Catholics from the urban core to the suburbs and from the Northeast and Upper Midwest to the West and Southwest.

The authors of the Notre Dame Study acknowledged that they neglected to address certain topics in sufficient detail. Among these topics were the following:

- The increase in the number of multicultural parishes, including increased numbers of Hispanic, Filipino, Korean, Vietnamese, and other parishioners, frequently within the same parish.

- The emerging forms of parish organizational structure, including multiparish ministry and parishes administered by someone who is not a priest.
- Parish finances, including the role of parish finance councils.
- The social ministry role of parishes.
- Adult catechesis. (Gremillion and Leege 1987: 25–27)

Many of the patterns identified in the Notre Dame Study have since intensified. This study intends to pick up where the Notre Dame Study left off, not only updating some of its findings but also examining some of the issues that the Notre Dame Study was not able to include.

PLAN FOR THE BOOK

As mentioned, the Notre Dame Study was a seminal work in the study of Catholic parishes. However, it is now almost 30 years old, and an update is sorely needed for much has changed in that time. Some of the topics it failed to cover have attained new significance and deserve an in-depth look. This book takes on both of those tasks.

Chapters 2 and 3 set the context for the rest of the book by examining the two most significant changes the Catholic Church in the United States has experienced in the past 30 years: the changing parish and changing clergy demographics. They underlie nearly every facet of 21st-century parish life.

As chapter 2 notes, U.S. Catholic parishes are far more multicultural than they were 30 years ago, due to the influx of parishioners from across the globe. It is not unheard of for a single parish to serve a diverse group of parishioners, possibly speaking ten or more languages and representing at least as many cultural traditions. The balance of generational cohorts in many parishes has also shifted, often depending on the parish's geographic location. For example, many inner-city parishes have lost nearly all but the oldest generation of parishioners as the younger generations have moved to the suburbs. At the same time there have been regional shifts in the U.S. Catholic population out of the Northeast and Upper Midwest and into the South and Southwest. As a result many parishes in decline have closed or been merged with other parishes, creating larger and more complex parishes.

Along with these changes is a noticeable change in the personnel leading parishes. Chapter 3 documents that there are fewer priests available to serve in parishes and that the priesthood in general is aging. Many dioceses have found the need to supplement their core of diocesan priests by recruiting international priests, many with language and cultural challenges. The growth of the permanent diaconate has also helped to expand and diversify the ministry of the Word and sacraments.

Chapters 4 and 5 discuss parish structures and administration. Chapter 4 examines options available in canon law to find innovative parish staffing structures that offer new opportunities for pastoral leadership. These include utilizing a team of priests (canon 517.1); assigning a nonpriest (deacon or lay person) administrator, typically called a parish life coordinator, to a parish (canon 517.2); and assigning one priest to pastor more than one parish (canon 526). Finally, parishes can be merged, creating even larger parishes. All of these options have their strengths and weaknesses.

Regardless of how a parish is staffed, it must be administered, and chapter 5 considers various parish administrative issues. Canon law places the responsibility for administering both the pastoral and temporal aspects of a Catholic parish squarely with the pastor. However, that doesn't preclude the pastor from delegating some of this responsibility to a parish business manager or other parish staff. Parish advisory councils, such as parish pastoral councils and finance councils, are available to advise the pastor. Some pastors are more effective than others at taking advantage of these options.

Chapters 6 through 9 take an in-depth look at parish life. Chapter 6 examines the current state of parish finances from a variety of perspectives, including the sources of revenue and the types of costs incurred. In addition to these bottom-line concerns, the chapter addresses the unease over the state of internal financial controls in light of the spate of parish embezzlements and corresponding parishioner demands for improved financial transparency and accountability.

Chapter 7 provides a look at contemporary Catholic parishioners. It compares parishioner demographics from current research to the characteristics of parishioners reported in the Notre Dame Study and illustrates graphically some of these changes, including in marital status, education, and parish engagement. The chapter describes a typical parishioner compared to 30 years ago.

Chapter 8 examines the multicultural reality of parish life. This includes an examination of parishes that have a particular ethnic ministry as well as parishes that are intentionally multicultural in their mission and ministry.

Chapter 9 describes the experience and opinions of Catholics in the pews. Important liturgical issues such as the type of music being played, the quality of the homilies, and reactions to liturgical change are examined. Parishioners describe what attracts them to their parish and evaluate their parish according to nine essential elements of parish life. The chapter also investigates parishioner attitudes about the types and quality of parish programs and services. These include the various parish ministries and community-building outreach activities, such as evangelization and communication.

Chapter 10 serves as a summary chapter, reviewing the various trends that have been identified throughout the book and examining the impact these trends have had on parish life.

DATA SOURCES

The data supporting the analysis in this book are primarily drawn from a variety of surveys conducted by CARA in recent years. More specifics on the data resulting from the Emerging Models Project, along with a description of other data sets used throughout this book, can be found in the appendix.

CONCLUSION

The Notre Dame Study of Catholic Parish Life was a groundbreaking look at U.S. Catholic parishes. However, Catholic parish life in the United States has experienced many dramatic changes in the intervening years, so the study's results needs to be updated.

This book employs data from a variety of recently completed studies to both update and in many ways expand on the Notre Dame Study. As was true in that study the data include not only factual information but also parishioner opinions on parish activities and cover virtually every aspect of parish life. Also like the Notre Dame Study our findings will surprise many and hopefully contribute to the conversation about the way parishes can better serve their members and the wider parish community.

CHAPTER TWO

A QUARTER-CENTURY OF CHANGE

Over the first half of the 20th century, the Catholic population in the United States grew steadily at approximately 2 to 4 percent per year. Between 1900 and 1950 the number of Catholics in the United States had increased from just over 10 million to just under 30 million, an increase of 165 percent. That growth slowed gradually, to about 1 to 2 percent annually, over the course of the second half of the century, while still keeping pace with overall U.S. population growth. At the dawn of the 21st century U.S. Catholics numbered well over 70 million. Modest projections suggest that number could approach 100 million by the middle of this century.

The proportion of Catholics has been steady at about a quarter of the adult population of the United States since the end of World War II, although that stability masks tremendous change in demographics. Much of that change has occurred just in the past quarter-century.

POPULATION GROWTH AND DISPERSION

The increase in Catholic population in the 19th century and first half of the 20th century was primarily due to immigration from Europe and rapid growth in the number of U.S. Catholic families. By the middle of the 20th century the country's nearly 30 million Catholics were still concentrated in the Northeast and Midwest and were just beginning to grow out of the traditional immigrant population settlement patterns that had so marked the Catholic experience in the United States of that era.

In the mid-1980s, when the Notre Dame Study was under way, about 52 million Catholic parishioners were served by more than 19,000 parishes in the 185 Catholic dioceses whose bishops belonged to the U.S. Conference of Catholic Bishops. These parishes, and the Catholic population as a whole, were struggling to cope with rapid demographic pressures affecting all Americans after World War II, but perhaps Catholics more than most. Catholics were succeeding in U.S. society well beyond the expectations and aspirations of their immigrant forebears. The GI Bill, a strong economy, and an immigrant work ethic all helped propel the children and grandchildren of Catholic immigrants into good schools, good jobs, and good neighborhoods. These children and grandchildren of immigrants moved out of the inner-city immigrant neighborhoods of the Northeast and into the suburbs. They moved off the immigrant farms of the Midwest and into major metropolitan areas of the South and West, where the jobs were located. For a time many of them returned to the old neighborhood for Sunday Mass and dinner with the grandparents, but that became harder to achieve as family and work conflicts drew people farther away. Eventually the old immigrant parishes became harder to sustain as their Catholic population moved away or died.

By the mid-1980s this enormous change in where Catholics live was just beginning to be felt. Some people found that the old inner-city ethnic neighborhoods were transforming from Irish Catholic, Italian Catholic, and Polish Catholic into a broader mix of cultures. New immigrant populations, many of them non-Catholic, were supplanting the dense Catholic populations of the inner cities. At the same time the suburbs around major cities were booming, with Catholic families adding pressure for new parishes and new schools, particularly in the rapidly growing metro areas of the South and the West. With the exception of French Catholic southern Louisiana and parts of Texas, New Mexico, Arizona, and southern California that were Mexican before they were American, these regions had never had sizable Catholic populations and struggled to keep up with the demand.

By 2010 a mere quarter-century after the Notre Dame Study, Catholics were almost equally distributed among the four census

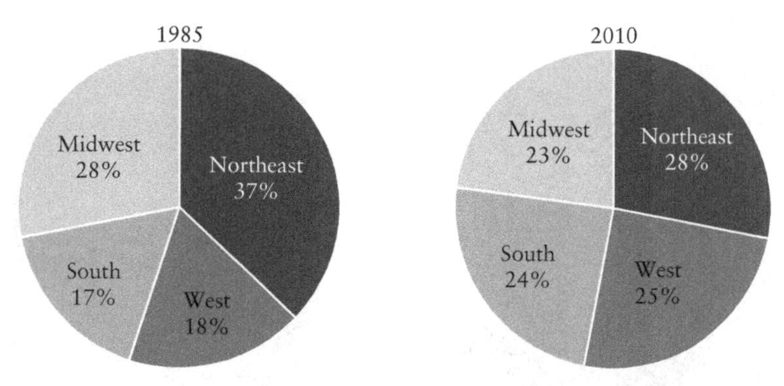

Figure 2.1 Regional Distribution of Catholic Population, 1985–2010.
Source: *The Official Catholic Directory*, relevant years.

regions, with just a little more than a quarter of the population living in the Northeast, where most of the Catholic infrastructure (parishes and schools, colleges, seminaries) is still concentrated (see Figure 2.1). Much of the growth of Catholic population in the South and West is due to internal migration, as the urban areas in the Northeast and rural areas of the Midwest lose younger Catholics to jobs in the Sunbelt and in the suburbs around major metropolitan areas. Some of the additional growth, particularly in the South and the West, is due to the in-migration of Hispanic Catholics from Latin America.

The U.S. Catholic population has realigned itself in the course of a few generations. People move, but parishes and schools do not. The map in Figure 2.2 shows even more clearly this growth in the West and the South and its corresponding impact on parishes. Bishops in the Northeast gradually came to accept the realization that the infrastructure of parishes and schools that had nurtured and supported generations of Catholic immigrants were no longer sustainable. Seven dioceses in the Northeast experienced a net loss of 50 or more parishes each between 2000 and 2010, including Buffalo, New York; Scranton, Pennsylvania; Boston, Massachusetts; Portland, Maine; Cleveland, Ohio; Albany, New York; and Rochester, New York. Each of these dioceses also experienced a loss in their Catholic population of between 8 and 16 percent during that same 10-year period.

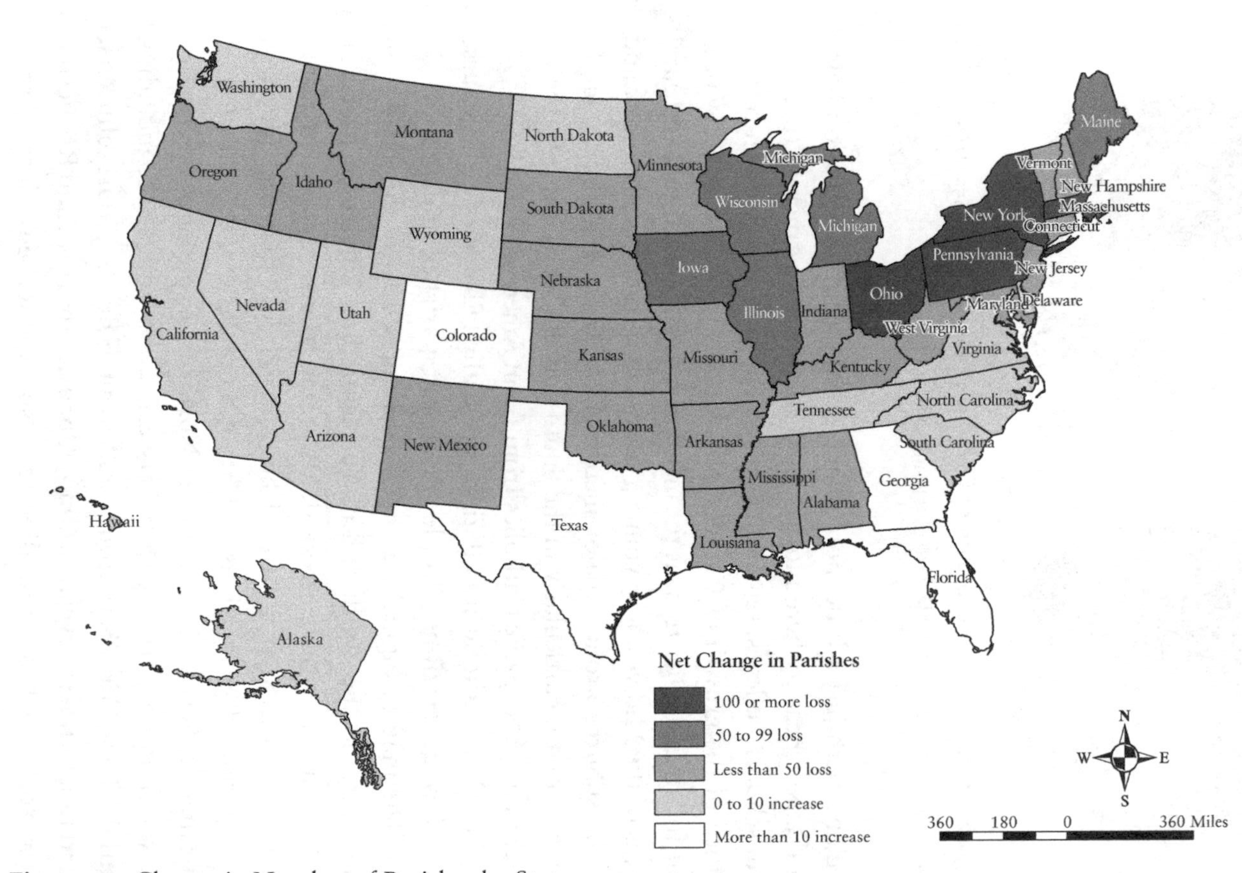

Figure 2.2 Change in Number of Parishes by State, 2000–2010.

Source: The Official Catholic Directory, relevant years.

Meanwhile the archdiocese of Atlanta added 10 new parishes between 2000 and 2010, but even that rate of construction could not keep up with the demand, as its total Catholic population increased 259 percent in the decade. Even with 10 new parishes, the archdiocese had more than 10,000 Catholics per parish in 2010.

The diocese of Buffalo, which had closed 97 parishes after losing 90,000 Catholics between 2000 and 2010, saw the number of Catholics per parish rise to 3,750 in 2010, when the national average was 3,500—an increase of 17 percent from 2000. The increase in Catholics per parish was due to parish closures, however, not due to any net increase in the number of Catholics.

ETHNIC AND CULTURAL CHANGE

Unlike the earlier waves of Catholic immigrants, who came predominantly from western and southern Europe, much of Catholic growth in the latter half of the 20th century was due to immigration from other Catholic populations around the world, such as Latin America, Vietnam, the Philippines, southern India, and the French- and English-speaking countries of Africa. Therefore the U.S. Catholic population today is quite ethnically and racially diverse. Just over half of all Catholics in the United States are non-Hispanic white, about four in ten are Hispanic/Latino, and the other 10 percent are non-Hispanic black, Asian, or Native American. This increased racial and ethnic diversity is most pronounced in regions of the country where the Catholic population is growing most rapidly, as can be seen in Figure 2.3.

In light of the fact that 30 years ago the Notre Dame Study did not consider it necessary to translate any of its survey materials into Spanish or any other language, the increase in racial and ethnic diversity is remarkable. In 1985 researchers from the Notre Dame Study estimated that "about 2,500 American parishes have Hispanic membership numerous enough to warrant use of their language during weekend Masses" (Gremillion and Leege 1987: 7). According to CARA research some 25 years later, more than 5,000 parishes now celebrate at least

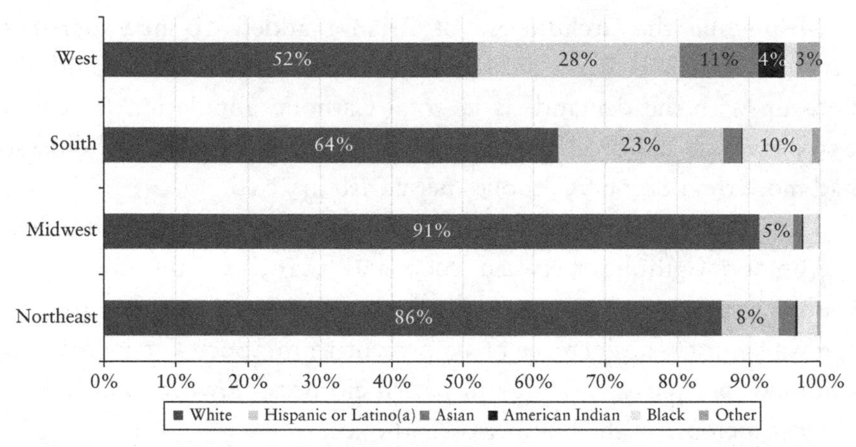

Figure 2.3 Race and Ethnicity of Registered Parishioners, by Region, 2010.
Source: Gray et al. 2011: 40.

one Mass a month in a language other than English; for 80 percent of those that language is Spanish. Some of the other languages used to celebrate Mass are Portuguese (6 percent of parishes), Vietnamese (2 percent), Italian (1 percent), Polish (1 percent), and American Sign Language (1 percent).

Of course language is only one aspect of culture. This increasing ethnic diversity also means that more and more parishes, particularly in the South and West, are evolving to incorporate the religious traditions of other Catholic cultures around the world, in music, in art, in recognition of other feast days and prayer practices, and in other ways. The ramifications for parish life are explored at more depth in chapters 7 and 9.

GENERATION AND ETHNICITY

Generational change is another significant difference in the Catholic population from the time of the Notre Dame Study. Generations are a useful way to categorize people according to the cultural forces that helped to shape their lives while they were growing up. Demographers regularly refer to the World War II generation as the group that came of age in the years preceding World War II and the baby boom generation as the very large group that was born in the prosperity years following that war. Similarly we use Catholic cultural markers to define Catholic generations according to the shared Catholic experiences that helped shaped individuals during their adolescence and early adult years:

- The pre–Vatican II generation was born in 1942 or earlier and roughly corresponds to the World War II generation. Its members all came of age before the Second Vatican Council and grew up with the Latin Mass said by the priest with his back to the people, in a largely immigrant, urban, working-class Catholic subculture that was struggling to assimilate into the larger American culture.
- The Vatican II generation are the baby boomers who were born between 1943 and 1960, a time of great demographic and economic growth in the United States. They came of age during the time of the Second Vatican Council, and their formative years likely spanned that time of profound changes in the Church.
- The post–Vatican II generation was born between 1961 and 1981. Sometimes called Generation X or baby busters, they have no lived experience of the pre–Vatican II Church. The best-educated generation ever, they are less likely than their parents to have attended a Catholic school.
- The millennial generation was born in 1982 or later. Sometimes called Generation Y, this group is even larger than the baby boomers. They came of age primarily under the papacies of John Paul II and Benedict XVI. Note that this generation, which now makes up a quarter of all adult Catholics, did not even exist at the time of the Notre Dame Study; the oldest of them would have been just three at the time.

As Figure 2.4 shows, about half of all adult Catholics at the time of the Notre Dame Study were Vatican II generation and nearly a third were pre–Vatican II generation. In our current investigation into Catholic parish life, the pre–Vatican II generation is just a tenth of all adult Catholics, and the two generations with no experience of a

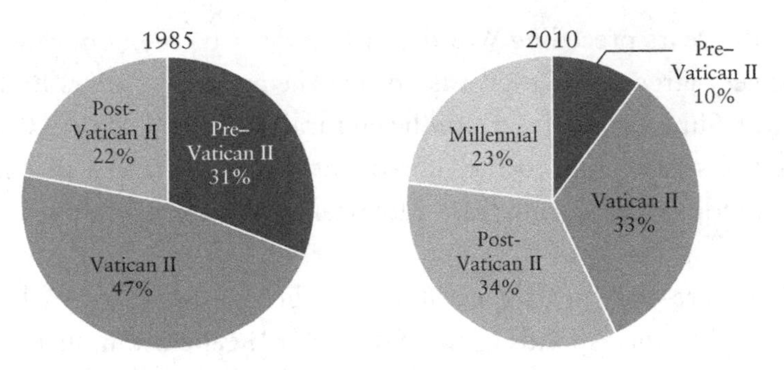

Figure 2.4 Catholic Generations, 1985–2010.

Source: D'Antonio et al. 2013: 33.

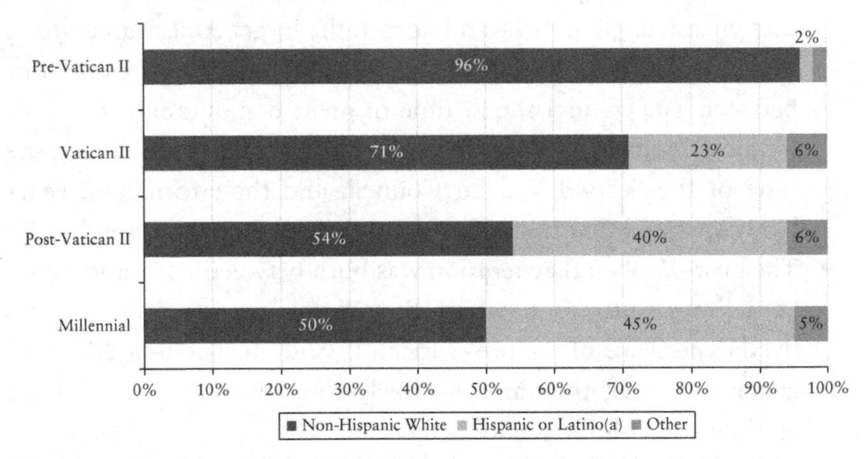

Figure 2.5 Racial and Ethnic Identification of Catholics by Generation, 2010.

Source: D'Antonio et al. 2013: 33.

pre–Vatican II church (post–Vatican II and millennial Catholics) now make up more than half of all adult Catholics. The changes in Catholic practice and belief that were beginning to be noticed by the researchers at Notre Dame have continued apace and are explored at more depth in later chapters.

When we compare these four generations of Catholics according to their ethnicity, we see even more clearly how racial and ethnic diversity is changing the face of the Church (see Figure 2.5). Post–Vatican II and millennial Catholics, who now make up more than half of all Catholics, are almost equal proportions non-Hispanic white and

Hispanic or other race or ethnicity (such as African American, Asian American, Native American). Thus generational change and increased ethnic and racial diversity together signify some of the incredible diversity in parish life and practice explored here.

PARISH SIZE AND DISTRIBUTION

As church leaders struggle to cope with these changing population demographics they must also deal with a mismatch between supply and demand. Bishops have to balance the need for parishes and schools to serve their Catholic population with the reality of limited financial resources and a diminished supply of clergy. In the past decade, for example, through a combination of closings and mergers, Church leaders have reduced the number of Catholic parishes in the United States by 1,359 (a decline of 7.1 percent). In 2000 the United States had more than 19,000 Catholic parishes; by decade's end there were fewer than 17,800, almost the same number it had in 1965 (see Figure 2.6).

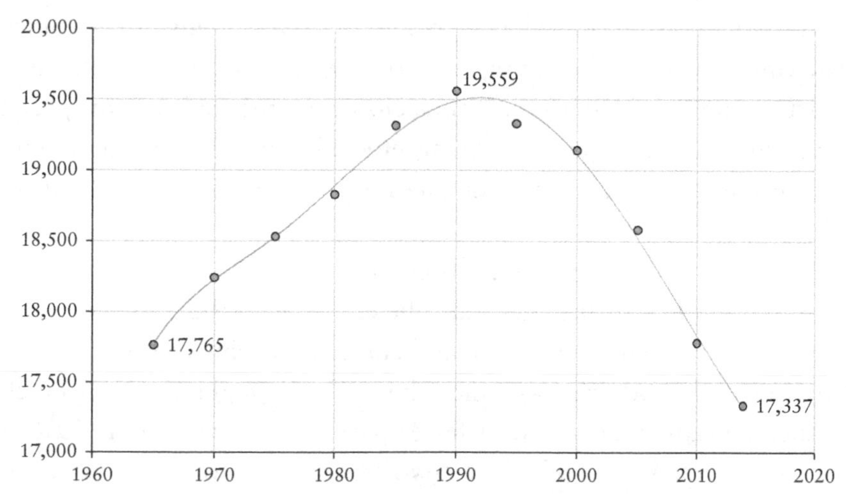

Figure 2.6 Number of Parishes in the United States, 1965–2010.
Source: Gray et al. 2011: 6.

These closures are concentrated in areas of the United States where waves of Catholic immigrants created parishes in the 19th and 20th centuries. Those parishes were often erected in the urban centers, where the immigrant populations had settled in order to meet the needs of those specific ethnic and language groups. In the 21st century the distribution of the Catholic population is no longer closely aligned with these parishes, as we described earlier. Many of these older parishes, built a century ago for an immigrant Catholic population that has assimilated and moved on, are crumbling and in need of extensive repair. While they still have nostalgic and perhaps historic value, the cost of upkeep can no longer be shouldered by their dwindled and aged congregation nor justified as an expense for the diocese to take on. Dioceses struggle to balance the desire to respect the historical patrimony of the existing structures with the very real demand for new parishes and schools in areas where the population is growing.

About a third of all U.S. Catholic parishes in existence today were established after 1950, and just one in ten has been established since 1976. In other words, even after all the parish closures, two out of three parishes in existence today were built to meet the needs of the pre–Vatican II church.

As recently as the mid-1980s, during the time of the Notre Dame Study, more parishes were being erected than were being closed. Since that time, however, the supply side of the equation has diminished, and the number of parishes being closed or merged has outpaced the number of new parishes being erected. (We discuss the supply side of the parish equation—finances and clergy—in more depth in chapter 3.)

The newer churches that have been built, especially in the South and West, tend to be much larger than the churches in the Northeast and in the Midwest that are merging and closing. The churches built in the 19th and early 20th century, when the Catholic population was much smaller, typically seated 500 or fewer parishioners. More than half of the Catholic churches built since 1950 seat 500 or more, and a quarter of the new parishes constructed since 2001 seat 1,000 or more (see Figure 2.7).

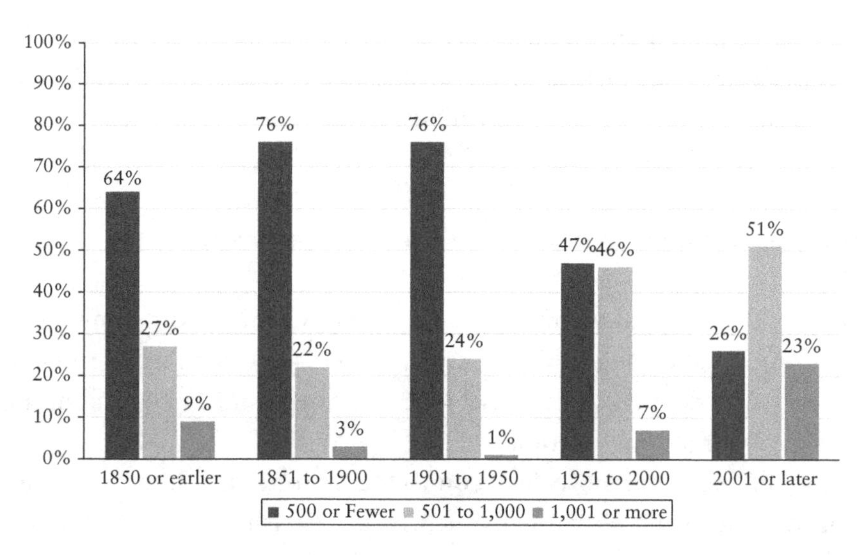

Figure 2.7 Parish Seating by Year of Building.
Source: Gray, et al. 2011.

Even with these much larger buildings, parishes must offer multiple weekend Masses to accommodate all the people. The average Catholic church is filled to 47 percent of parish capacity over the course of a weekend, including all Saturday vigil and Sunday Masses. On average, parishes offer about four Masses per weekend; 10 percent offer just one Sunday Mass on a weekend, but 28 percent celebrate five or more Masses per weekend.

The Notre Dame Study estimated that 18 percent of Catholic parishes had fewer than 500 parishioners; 28 percent served between 500 and 1,499; 17 percent had between 1,500 and 2,499; 22 percent served between 2,500 and 5,000; and 16 percent had more than 5,000 parishioners. The average parish in that study had 2,300 registered parishioners (Gremillion and Castelli 1987: 53). Twenty-five years later the Emerging Models Study found that the average parish had nearly 3,300 registered parishioners. This represents a 39 percent increase in parish size over this quarter-century. Some 16 percent of parishes in the Emerging Models Study are small, with 430 or fewer registered parishioners; 20 percent have between 431 and 1,200 parishioners; about 30 percent have between 1,201 and 3,000; and more than 35 percent serve over 3,000 parishioners. Is there an upper limit to parish size? In fact the average multicultural parish in the Emerging Models Study had more than 4,000 registered parishioners.[1]

MEMBERSHIP AND PARISH SHOPPING

Needless to say, maintaining a strong sense of Catholic community and mission is challenging in these very large parish communities. In later chapters we describe how parishioners connect and find meaning in these very large congregations.

Parishioners are now less connected to one another by neighborhood as well. Historically nearly all parishes had geographic boundaries, and Catholics were expected to attend the parish within whose territory they lived. At the time of the Notre Dame Study about 85 percent of Catholics attended the parish where they lived; the other 15 percent crossed boundaries to attend a parish they preferred. In the Emerging Models Study more than 30 percent of parishioners report that they drive past a parish closer to their home in order to attend Mass at a parish they prefer. This is more common among nonwhite parishioners and among younger parishioners. More than half of African American parishioners and close to half of Asian American and Hispanic parishioners drive past parishes closer to their home to attend Mass. About two-fifths of millennials and more than a third of post–Vatican II generation parishioners say they too drive past a parish closer to home to attend Mass at a parish of their choice.

1. In the Emerging Models Study multicultural parishes are defined as meeting at least one of three criteria: (1) regularly celebrating Mass in a language other than English (or Latin); (2) the percentage of parishioners who are non-Hispanic white is less than 40 percent; or (3) the diversity index is 33 percent or higher. The diversity index measures the probability that two randomly selected parishioners in a parish would be of a different race or ethnicity. In many cases the parishes identified as multicultural met more than one of these criteria.

CONCLUSION

We have seen some dramatic change in Catholic population trends since the Notre Dame Study. Most notably Catholics have grown out of the predominantly white, mostly European immigrant subculture that so strongly identified them through the middle of the 20th century. They have also left the immigrant neighborhoods behind; as the children and grandchildren of those immigrants they have moved up and out, socioeconomically, to take jobs and raise families. As they did so the infrastructure they left behind, such as inner-city parishes and schools in the Northeast and Upper Midwest, have been merging and closing as bishops cope with decreasing funds and fewer priests. Gradually newer and larger parishes are being built in the suburbs around major cities, largely in the South and the West, to meet the demand of an increasing Catholic population.

This expanding Catholic population is also becoming more racially and ethnically diverse, as Hispanic Catholics now make up approximately half of the Catholic population under age 50. At the same time increasing numbers of immigrant Catholics from Asia, Africa, and the Pacific add to the diversity of the Church in the United States.

One reason parishes tend to be larger today and fewer in number than they were at the time of the Notre Dame Study is because the number of priests has not kept pace with the increase in the Catholic population. The next chapter discusses key trends in clergy demographics and changes in pastoral leadership during the time between these two studies that have had a major impact on the size, structure, and functioning of parish life in the United States.

CHAPTER THREE

CHANGING DEMOGRAPHICS IN PASTORAL LEADERSHIP

TRENDS AMONG PRIESTS

While the trend in U.S. Catholic population over the past quarter-century has been toward growth, movement, and increasing diversity, the overall trend among priests has been toward an aging population and decreased numbers. The total number of Catholic priests in the United States peaked in 1969 and has been declining steadily since that time (see Figure 3.1). This is largely a function of an earlier trend, one that occurred more than fifty years ago.

After World War II, from the mid-1940s through the mid-1960s, seminaries welcomed hundreds of young Catholic men each year who were pursuing a vocation to priesthood. These two decades proved exceptional, though, and seminary enrollments have dropped steadily since the late 1960s. As a result this very large cohort of priests who were ordained as young men in the 1960s and 1970s are now entering their 70s and 80s and are retiring from active ministry. The much smaller ordination cohorts that followed have not been sufficient in number to compensate for the numbers that left, retired, or died.

We experience this diminishment as a "shortage of priests," although no other world region except for Europe has as favorable a ratio of Catholics per priest as the United States. In 2013 the Vatican reported just over 3,000 Catholics per priest worldwide. Africa and the Americas each have nearly 5,000, Asia and Oceania have a little over 2,000, and Europe overall has just over 1,500 Catholics per priest. By comparison

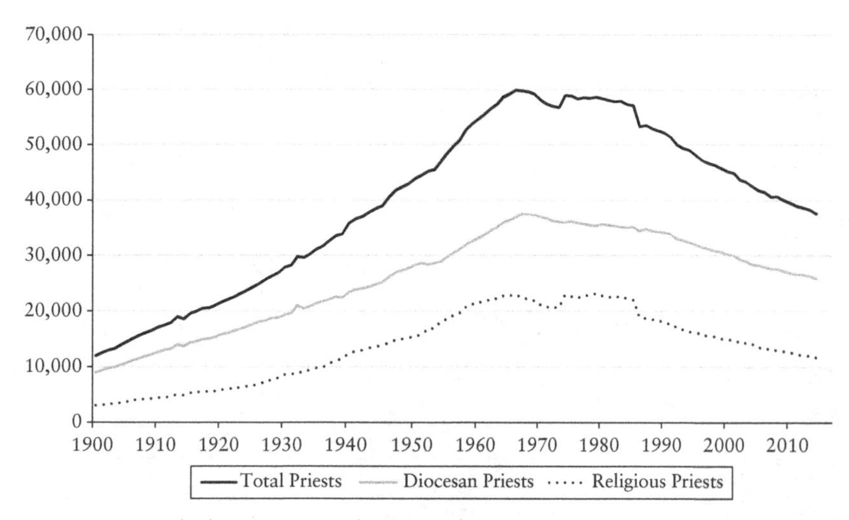

Figure 3.1 Catholic Priests in the United States: 1900–2010.
Source: *The Official Catholic Directory*, relevant years.

the United States has just over 1,700 Catholics per priest. A shortage for us in the United States, yes, but largely due to the lingering effects of an extraordinary period in U.S. Catholic history.

CATHOLICS PER PRIEST

The number of Catholics in the United States has increased steadily over the course of the 20th century, as described in chapter 2. The increase remains at about 1 percent per year into the 21st century due to the twin forces of natural increase and immigration. The total number of priests kept up with and even outpaced Catholic population growth in the first half of the 20th century, which can be seen by the downward trend in the line signifying Catholics per priest in Figure 3.2.

For a couple of decades around midcentury the supply of priests was sufficient enough that many priests served in a wide variety of apostolates beyond or in addition to parish ministry. Nearly every parish had a resident priest, and many had at least a couple of associates—younger

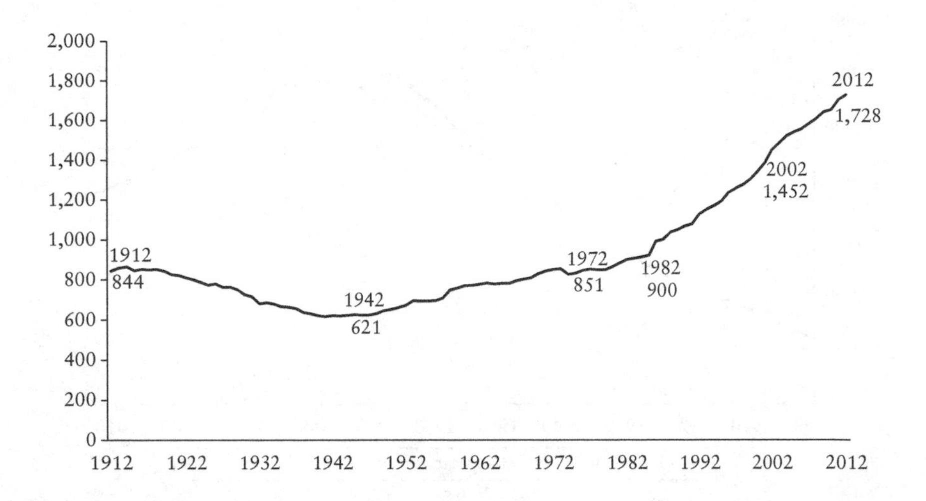

Figure 3.2 Catholics per Priest, 1912–2012.
Source: *The Official Catholic Directory*, relevant years.

priests in residence, gaining experience as they worked in parish ministry while they waited to be appointed pastor in a parish of their own.

This scenario changed gradually in the 1960s and 1970s as the supply of priests no longer kept pace with the growth in Catholic population. By the time of the Notre Dame Study in the mid-1980s, the authors were already describing a priest shortage (Gremillion and Castelli 1987: 28), which has only increased with the passage of time. There are now twice as many Catholics per priest nationally as there were at the time of the Notre Dame Study, and this trend line will continue its upward arc at least into the near future as the numbers of men being ordained each year are insufficient to keep up with the growth in Catholic population.

NUMBERS OF SEMINARIANS IN FORMATION

The overall numbers of seminarians in formation at the graduate level for priestly ministry in the United States declined by half from the mid-1960s through the mid-1980s, but the decline has tapered off since that

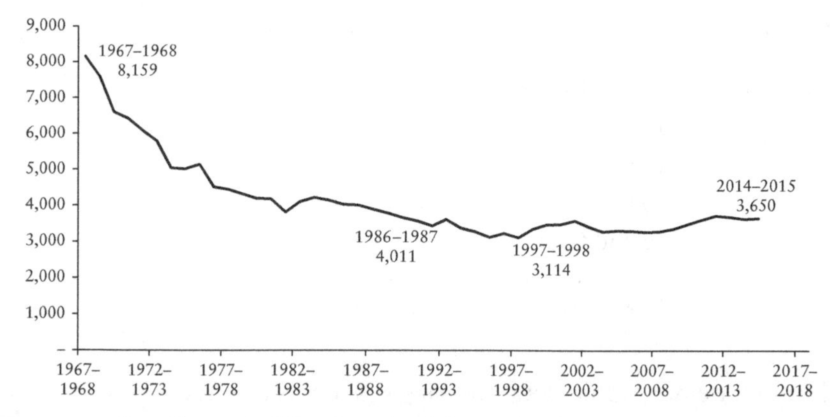

Figure 3.3 Enrollment in Theology in U.S. Seminaries.

Source: Gautier et al. 2015.

time and has even begun a slight increase since the low point in the mid-1990s (see Figure 3.3).

The positive message here is that there is a steady supply of future priests in the pipeline, between 3,000 and 4,000 men in formation each year at the graduate level. This results in about 450 to 550 new priests ordained each year for ministry in the United States. However, the sobering reality is that this is only about a third the number needed to compensate for the large numbers of elderly priests who are dying, retiring, or otherwise leaving pastoral ministry. And this does not take into account the other reality: that the Catholic population in the United States is continuing to increase at about 1 percent per year. Needless to say the perceived shortage of priests that we experience in the United States is a fact of life that will be with us into the future.

AGES OF PRIESTS AND SEMINARIANS

The large cohort of priests that were ordained in the 1960s and 1970s is also reflected in the average age of priests over time. For example, researchers report that the average age of priests overall in the United States in the 1970s was mid-30s (Greeley 1972); in the 1990s it was mid-50s; and by the 2000s it was mid-60s (Gautier et al. 2012).

Table 3.1 Ages of Priests in Parish Ministry

39 and Under	11%
40 to 49	17
50 to 59	25
60 to 69	30
70 and Older	17

Source: Emerging Models Study, parish survey.

Although demographic data on priests, such as age and ethnicity, were not reported in the Notre Dame Study, we do have such data from the parishes surveyed in the Emerging Models Study. Nearly half of the priests staffing these parishes surveyed in 2010 are 60 or older (see Table 3.1).

The current age distribution of priests in parish ministry is a function of three primary factors:

- *Good health*. Most priests in parish ministry today were ordained for ministry 30, 40, or even 50 years ago and continue to serve as priests in parishes. Like most Americans, they are living longer and enjoying good health that allows an active lifestyle well into their 70s and even 80s. As the Catholic population continues to increase and the supply of younger, newly ordained priests remains low, these priests respond to the need for sacramental ministers by their continued service as pastors or pastoral associates. In fact the Emerging Models data on parish leaders reveal that one in four priests over the age of 60 who are serving as pastors or pastoral associates are ministering in multiple parish settings (canon 526.1). The increasing shortage of priests is resulting in more of these experienced priests being called upon to serve in more than one parish at a time.
- *Delayed retirement*. Every diocese allows for the retirement of priests, typically around age 70. Many priests continue in active ministry, although often in a reduced capacity, after they enter eligibility for retirement. CARA found, in a 2009 study of priests,

that 52 percent of diocesan priests and 58 percent of religious priests who have reached the age of retirement (which is 65 or older in the secular world) were still active in their ministry. Among all priests surveyed (regardless of age), just 15 percent were retired, and another 7 percent were semiretired (receiving at least partial retirement benefits). Often referred to as "senior priests," these men continue to provide vital sacramental and other pastoral ministry while typically being relieved of some of the administrative burden shouldered by younger priests (Gautier et al. 2012).

- *Later ordination.* As pastoral ministry becomes more complex and the number of men in formation for priestly ministry declines, the men who are being ordained priests are doing so later in life. In 1970, according to statistics reported to CARA by seminaries, high school seminaries enrolled about 12,000 young men who were considering a vocation to priesthood. The trajectory they followed typically included four years of college seminary (Gautier et al. 2012: 5). Today's vocation directors no longer encourage young men who are discerning a vocation to enter a seminary during high school; in fact high school seminaries have all but disappeared from the scene. More than 50 percent of the men being ordained today completed college before they entered the seminary. Another 15 percent entered the seminary with a graduate degree, often in a field other than theology or ministry. These men had to extend their priestly formation by an additional two years to attain the requisite philosophy foundation necessary for theology.

On average, men being ordained to priesthood in the 21st century are in their mid-30s at the time of their ordination (Gautier and Gaunt 2015). However, there is some evidence to suggest a bit of a reversal of this trend, as can be seen in Figure 3.4. Age data from the annual Catholic ministry formation statistics that CARA collects from seminaries show a recent trend toward a greater proportion of men in their 20s enrolled in theology, the graduate level of formation that culminates

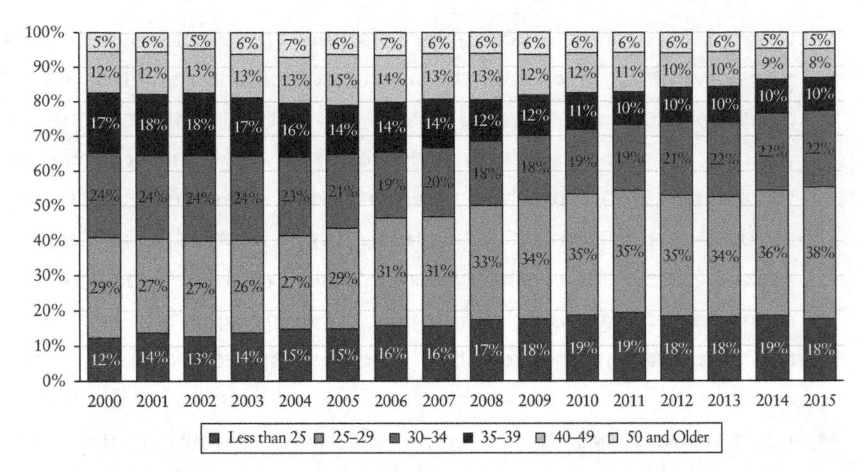

Figure 3.4 Age Distribution of Theologate Enrollment in U.S. Seminaries, 2000–2015.

Source: Gautier et al. 2015.

in ordination to priesthood. This trend, if it continues, will result in a slightly younger average age at ordination to priesthood.

RACIAL AND ETHNIC OR CULTURAL COMPOSITION OF PRIESTS

Although the U.S. Catholic population is ethnically and racially quite diverse, as was described in chapter 2, the priest population is less diverse, more reflective of the diversity seen in older generations of U.S. Catholics. So while just over 50 percent of all Catholics in the United States are non-Hispanic white, 81 percent of clergy leading parishes are non-Hispanic white (Figure 3.5).

Nevertheless the composition of parish priests in the Emerging Models staff dataset, reported by the more than 800 parishes that responded to the study's parish survey, is more diverse than was found in the survey of a national random sample of priests CARA conducted in 2009. That sample, which was not restricted to priests in parish ministry, was even less diverse: 92 percent were non-Hispanic white (Gautier et al. 2012: 10).

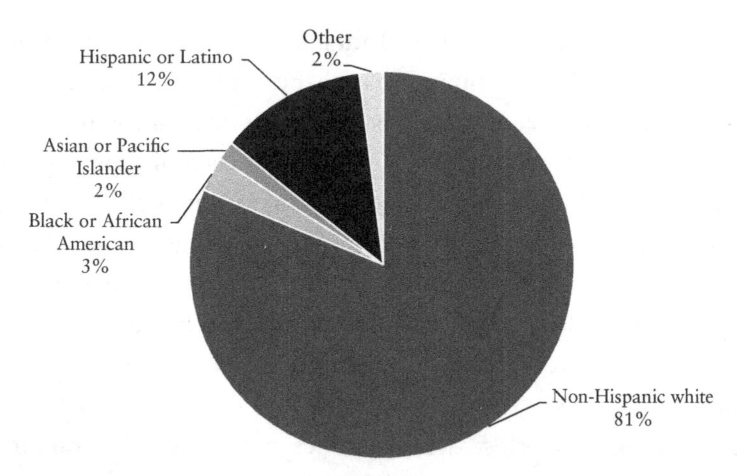

Figure 3.5 Race and Ethnicity of Parish Priests.
Source: Gray, et al. 2011.

One reason priests in parish ministry are more diverse than priests overall is because a large number of priests from outside the United States are ministering in U.S. parishes. Many bishops, facing an increasing number of Catholics and a declining number of available priests, have reached out to bishops and religious superiors in other countries to find priests who will minister in parishes in the United States. Although international priests ministering in the United States is not new (Smith 2004), the number of international priests and the number of countries from which they come have both increased in recent years.

When Andrew Greeley (1972) conducted his national sociological study of the priesthood for the U.S. Conference of Catholic Bishops (USCCB) in 1970, he reported that 11 percent of all diocesan priests in active ministry were born outside the United States—largely from Ireland or Germany. CARA also surveyed all U.S. dioceses in 1999 for the USCCB and again found that 11 percent of diocesan priests in active ministry were foreign-born. By this time, though, the largest sending countries were Ireland, India, the Philippines, Poland, Vietnam, and Mexico. In 2012, at the time of the Emerging Models Study, the USCCB was reporting more than 6,600 international priests serving in the United States, equal to one international priest for every four diocesan priests in active ministry (Gautier et al. 2014). The largest numbers of these priests now come from India, the Philippines, Nigeria, and Mexico, with a sizable remnant of Irish-born priests who came to the United States many years ago. Most of these international priests are not in the United States to serve the ministry needs of their own ethnic or language group, as was the case for many of the Irish, German, and Polish priests who came to this country a century ago to minister to the large immigrant Catholic population from their home country. Rather these priests must learn English (and often Spanish too) to minister in the increasingly diverse and complicated parishes to which they are assigned (Table 3.2).

These changes in priest demographics are being lived out in parishes across the United States. Today there are fewer priests overall than there were a generation ago; they are older and more diverse than priests of a generation ago; and the parishes in which they serve tend to be larger and much more complex. How do they do it? The next

Table 3.2 Numbers of International Priests by Country of Origin

Sending Country	1999	2008	2009	2010	2012
India	342	825	865	930	972
Philippines	327	706	687	686	702
Nigeria	101	522	565	566	616
Ireland	827	732	703	715	599
Mexico	224	473	426	496	505
Poland	256	346	396	428	455
Vietnam	231	354	299	342	366
Colombia	143	296	309	342	344
Spain	117	158	162	181	163
Sri Lanka	49	43	54	54	36
Other	874	1,518	1,673	1,803	1,859
Year Total	**3,491**	**5,973**	**6,139**	**6,543**	**6,617**
International as percentage of all diocesan priests	**11%**	**22%**	**22%**	**24%**	**25%**

Sources: Froehle, Bendyna, and Gautier 1999; USCCB, Secretariat of Child and Youth Protection (2008–2012 data).

chapter describes parish staffing trends and the ways parishes are making do with fewer priests. First, though, we describe other parish ministry staff and examine the trends over time among each: permanent deacons, religious brothers and sisters, and lay ecclesial ministers.

TRENDS AMONG PERMANENT DEACONS

A permanent deacon is an ordained member of the clergy with a special ministry of service (called *diakonia*). Permanent deacons are not priests, but they can perform many of the sacramental ministries of a priest, including baptizing and witnessing marriages as well as preaching homilies. Unlike a priest they cannot consecrate the Eucharist or hear confessions.

The Notre Dame Study found one in four parishes have a permanent deacon assigned to the parish (Gremillion and Castelli 1987: 56), as these pastoral ministers were just coming onto the scene in the mid-1980s. The number of permanent deacons in the United States has grown steadily, though, since the restoration of this ministry in the years following the Second Vatican Council. In 2000 CARA's *National Parish Inventory* reported that one in three parishes had at least one permanent deacon (Gautier and Perl 2000). In the 2010 parish survey that was part of the Emerging Models Study four in ten parishes reported at least one permanent deacon among their parish staff (Figure 3.6). Thus as the number of priests diminishes and as bishops are closing parishes in areas of declining Catholic population, permanent deacons are emerging as an increasing presence in parish life today.

According to numbers reported in *The Official Catholic Directory*, in 2014 the United States had more than 18,000 permanent deacons. The number of permanent deacons has increased by approximately 3 percent per year over each of the previous 10 years. In fact if current trends continue, the total number of permanent deacons is likely to surpass the total number of diocesan priests in the next few years.

We are particularly aware of this trend because CARA also monitors enrollment in the 175 diaconate formation programs offered in the

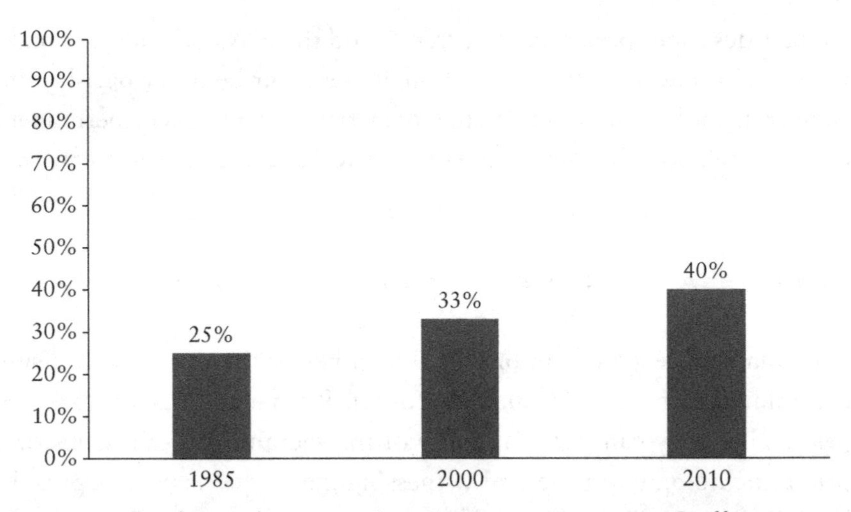

Figure 3.6 Parishes with at Least One Permanent Deacon on Staff.

Sources: Gautier and Perl 2000; Gray, et al. 2011; Gremillion and Castelli 1987 (for 1985 data).

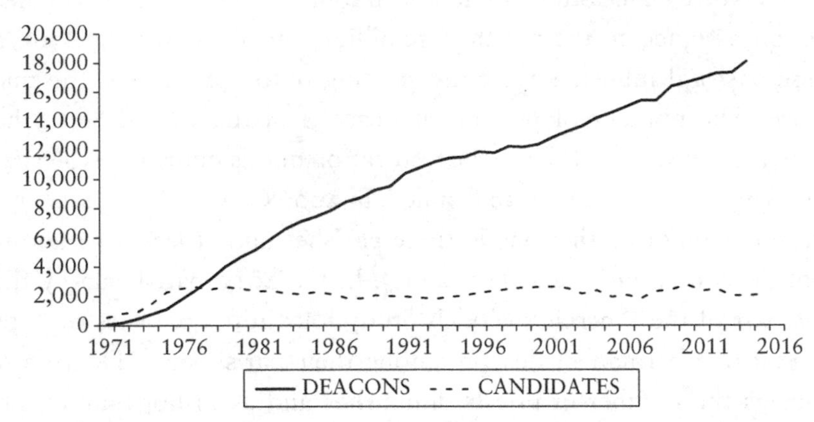

Figure 3.7 Deacons and Deacon Candidates, 1971–2015.

Source: Gautier et al. 2015.

United States and has documented approximately 2,000 men enrolled in formation each year for this ministry since the mid-1970s, as shown by the dashed line in Figure 3.7.

Unlike priests, permanent deacons can be married—and most of them are. Because these men cannot be accepted into formation for the diaconate until age 35, many have already served in a secular career before becoming deacons. Thus their average age is roughly equivalent to the average age of priests. Six in ten of the permanent deacons identified in the Emerging Models Study are 60 or older. Nevertheless they are an invaluable asset to the pastoral ministry of parishes and help moderate the effects of the priest shortage in parishes across the country.

Because they are approximately the same age as priests, on average, and therefore come from the same generation of older Catholics, deacons have a similar racial or ethnic profile as priests and other Catholics of their generation. However, a higher proportion of permanent deacons are Hispanic (12 percent) than is found in the population of priests (Figure 3.8). In fact one in five diaconate formation programs offers formation in both Spanish and English. Some programs provide separate English-language and Spanish-language tracks within the same program, and others conduct some of their classes for deacons in Spanish.

The deacons identified in the Emerging Models Study are found in parishes all across the country. About 25 percent are in parishes in the Northeast; 30 percent in the Midwest; not quite 20 percent in the West; and just over 25 percent in the South. Almost half of them serve in parishes that were identified as multicultural, according to the criteria established for the Emerging Models project (see the methodological appendix).

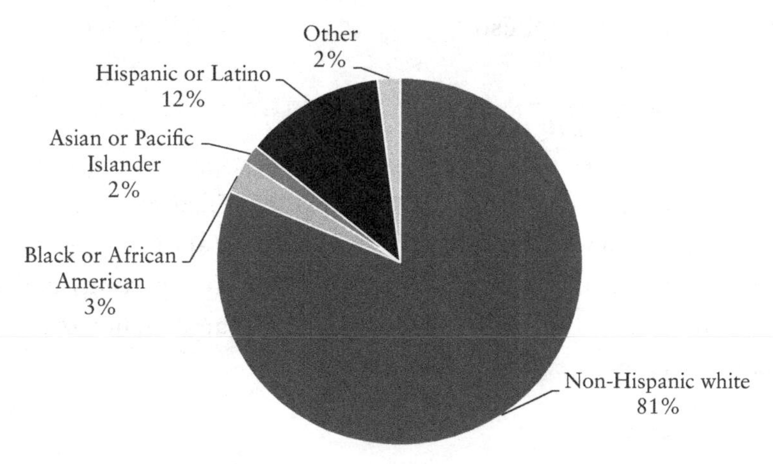

Figure 3.8 Race and Ethnicity of Permanent Deacons.

Source: Gray, et al. 2011.

WHAT DO DEACONS DO?

Permanent deacons are members of the clergy, ordained by their bishop for a ministry of service to the Church.[1] This service is wide-ranging and involves a great deal of quiet work with the poor and marginalized. Deacons are not financially compensated for this ministry of service, nor are they compensated for their liturgical ministry in parishes, which is where most people encounter them. The majority of permanent deacons are employed in a nonministry position outside the Church, or they have a working spouse who provides an income for their family, or they are receiving a retirement income from a secular occupation.

Nationally 18 percent of active permanent deacons are financially compensated for a ministry position that they fulfill in addition to their diaconal responsibilities (Gautier and Gaunt 2015). Nearly 30 percent of these deacons who are financially compensated are paid for a ministerial position they hold in a parish.

Outside of parish ministry about one in three deacons nationally who are financially compensated for their ministry are employed in prison ministry, hospital chaplaincy, diocesan ministry or administration, or ministry in a social services agency (Gautier and Gaunt 2015: 15). Most people, however, recognize deacons for their sacramental role in parish ministry.

PARISH MINISTRY OF DEACONS

Of the 846 parishes that responded to the first part of the Emerging Models Project, 345 parishes (41 percent) identified at least one permanent deacon among their parish staff, for a total of 594 permanent deacons. Most of these parishes with a deacon (60 percent) had just one deacon on the parish staff. A few very large parishes, however, have as many as seven or eight deacons on staff.

1. The word *diakonia*, from which the word *deacon* is derived, means "service" in Greek.

In addition to their diaconal responsibilities, about one in ten of these deacons are also employed by the parish in a variety of ministry positions. Some of the parish positions held by these permanent deacons are:

- Pastoral associate (also called pastoral assistant or pastoral minister)
- Parish life coordinator (canon 517.2)
- Business administrator, manager, or bookkeeper
- Director or coordinator of adult faith formation or Rite of Christian Initiation of Adults
- Catechetical ministry director or coordinator
- Youth ministry director
- Social ministry director
- Director of liturgy and music
- Facilities maintenance supervisor or coordinator

TRENDS AMONG RELIGIOUS SISTERS AND BROTHERS

Historically the trend lines for women religious and religious brothers in the United States have followed approximately the same trajectory as that for religious and diocesan priests. In other words, their numbers were very small through the 19th and early 20th century, increasing dramatically through the middle of the 20th century, then declining sharply after the late 1960s and continuing their downward trajectory since that time. Figure 3.9 displays the trend lines for diocesan and religious priests, permanent deacons, women religious, and brothers over this period. In 1969 the total size of this pastoral workforce was nearly a quarter million; by 2015 it was less than half that size, at just over 100,000.

The primary apostolates of women religious and religious brothers in the United States have been in teaching, hospital ministry, and social services, but these pastoral ministers have had a small but significant

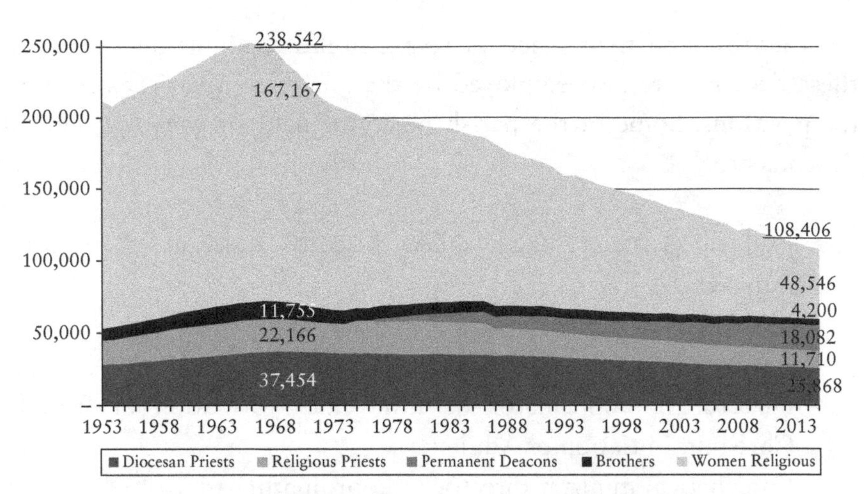

Figure 3.9 Ordained and Religiously Professed Men and Women, 1953–2015.
Source: *The Official Catholic Directory*, relevant years.

role in parish ministry in the United States throughout history. Sister Marie Augusta Neal (1984: 25) documents the presence of religious sisters in pastoral ministry in her book, *Catholic Sisters in Transition from the 1960s to the 1980s*. Her studies indicate that 2.9 percent of women religious were engaged in pastoral ministry work in 1966, more than doubling to 6 percent by 1982.

The Notre Dame Study reported that one-third of its parishes "have a religious sister hired explicitly for pastoral services, including 12 percent with more than one nun performing pastoral services. Only 5 percent of parishes have a brother employed in pastoral ministry" (Gremillion and Castelli 1987: 56). In 2000 CARA's *National Parish Inventory* (Gautier and Perl 2000) found that 29 percent of parishes had at least one woman religious on the parish staff. At that time 3 percent of parishes reported one or more religious brothers on the parish staff.

PARISH MINISTRY OF RELIGIOUS SISTERS AND BROTHERS

Of the 846 parishes that responded to Phase 1 of the Emerging Models Project, 149 (18 percent) identified at least one religious sister among their parish staff, for a total of 177 religious sisters. Most of these parishes with a sister (72 percent) had just one sister on the parish staff, and no parish reports more than four. Likewise 18 parishes (2 percent) identified at least one religious brother among their parish staff. A total of 22 religious brothers were identified by these parishes, and no parish reported more than three brothers on the parish staff.

The parish responsibilities of these religious vary widely. Eight percent of sisters engaged in parish ministry are parish life coordinators; that is, the bishop has entrusted the pastoral care of a parish to them due to a shortage of available priest pastors (canon 517.2). About four in ten women religious serving in parish ministry are a pastoral associate or pastoral minister. One in five is a director or coordinator of catechetical ministry for the parish. Others serve the parish in positions related to sacramental preparation, pastoral care, youth or senior ministry, liturgy, and music ministry. Among the religious brothers identified by these Emerging Models parishes as staff members, two are parish administrators and three are parish life coordinators. The others serve as pastoral associates, catechetical ministers, or in some other staff support role in the parish.

TRENDS AMONG LAY ECCLESIAL MINISTERS

Probably one of the most dramatic changes stemming from Vatican II that affected parish life in the United States was its call for an increased awareness among lay people of their co-responsibility with the clergy for parish life. As the *Decree on the Apostolate of the Lay People* (*Apostolicam Actuositatem*, paragraph 10) stated, "Sharing in the function of Christ, priest, prophet and king, the laity have an active part of their own in the life and activity of the church. Their activity within the church communities is so necessary that without it the apostolate of the pastors will frequently be unable to obtain its full effect" (Second Vatican Council 1965). Lay people responded to that call in amazing numbers.

Although lay people have always been an important source of volunteer service in parishes, they did not commonly serve in paid positions as parish pastoral staff until after Vatican II. The definition of lay ecclesial ministers outlined in *Co-Workers in the Vineyard of the Lord*

(U.S. Conference of Catholic Bishops 2005) describes these individuals as adequately formed and prepared lay persons, authorized by the hierarchy to serve publicly in leadership for a particular area of ministry, in close mutual collaboration with clergy. The estimated number of lay ecclesial ministers serving in U.S. parishes surpassed the number of diocesan priests in the early 2000s. The most recent estimate, from the Emerging Models data, counts nearly 40,000 providing lay ecclesial ministry for the Catholic Church in the United States.

The Notre Dame Study did not attempt to estimate the number of lay ministers serving in U.S. parishes, but it did report that 30 percent of U.S. parishes "employ lay persons specifically for pastoral ministry—remarkably, about the same percentage hiring nuns [*sic*] for such roles. One-third of the parishes with lay ministers have more than one, including 4 percent who report having five or more" (Gremillion and Castelli 1987: 56).

The first systematic national study of lay ecclesial ministry was carried out in 1990 by the late Msgr. Philip Murnion at the request of the USCCB. Murnion (1992) surveyed 1,163 parishes in 43 randomly selected dioceses. From the data reported by these parishes he estimated that there were 21,569 "lay parish ministers" in the United States, defined as paid, nonordained parish ministry staff working at least 20 hours per week. These lay ecclesial ministers included religious sisters and brothers as well as other lay persons. Among them 41 percent were vowed religious (nearly all sisters, with fewer than 1 percent religious brothers) and 59 percent other lay persons.

In 1997 Murnion and David DeLambo replicated the 1990 study with a survey of 949 parishes in the same 43 dioceses. This study estimated that the number of lay ecclesial ministers had increased to 29,146, an increase of 35 percent in just five years. This study also defined "lay parish ministers" as religious sisters and brothers as well as other lay persons, working at least 20 hours per week in a paid parish ministry position (Murnion and DeLambo 1999). In 2005 DeLambo replicated the two previous national studies with a survey of 929 parishes in the same 43 dioceses. This study estimated that there were 30,632 "lay parish ministers" in ministry in the United States.

CARA's estimates for the current number of lay ecclesial ministers serving in parishes is based on the parish survey from the Emerging Models Study. The sample included parishes in all U.S. territorial dioceses and utilized a grid design that was very similar to that used by DeLambo to request information from respondents about the parish staff. This study estimates that there were 37,929 lay ecclesial ministers in parish pastoral ministry in the United States in 2010. Just under half of lay ecclesial ministers had a graduate or professional degree (46 percent); 60 percent had attended Catholic primary schools; 47 percent had been enrolled in a Catholic secondary school; and 58 percent had attended a Catholic college or university. Only 5 percent of these lay ecclesial ministers were under the age of 30; about 40 percent were under the age of 50; and a majority, 62 percent, were 50 or older (Table 3.3).

Table 3.3 The Changing Profile of Lay Ecclesial Ministers

	2012	2005	1999	1990
Number of lay ecclesial ministers	37,929	30,632	29,146	21,569
Gender				
Male	20%	20%	15%	18%
Female	80%	80%	85%	82%
Race/Ethnicity				
Non-Hispanic white	88%	89%	94%	–
Hispanic/Latino(a)	9%	8%	4%	–
African American	1.6%	1.4%	1.2%	–
Asian/Pacific Islander	1.7%	1.7%	0.6%	–
Native American	0.2%	0.1%	0.1%	–
Median age	55	64	61	58
Ecclesial Status				
Vowed religious	14%	16%	28%	41%
Other lay person	86%	84%	72%	59%
Graduate or professional degree	46%	48%	42%	53%

Sources: DeLambo 2005; Gray 2012; Murnion 1992; Murnion and DeLambo 1999.

The trend over time since 1992 indicates that, on average, about 790 new lay ecclesial ministers are added to U.S. parish ministry staffs per year. Overall we expect that the growth in rate of increase has slowed from the five-year pace between 1992 and 1997 but the number of lay ecclesial ministers continues to grow just as the number of priests and vowed religious who are available for ministry becomes smaller each year. CARA estimates there are currently about 40,000 lay ecclesial ministers serving in parish ministry.

Table 3.4 puts the race and ethnicity of lay ecclesial ministers into the broader context of the workforce of the Catholic Church and the

Table 3.4 Race and Ethnicity within the U.S. Catholic Church

	White	Hispanic	Black	Asian	Other
Clergy					
Catholic priests	92%	3%	2%	3%	<1%
Catholic priests born after 1960	75	15	2	8	<1
Permanent deacons (active)	76	16	4	3	1
Ordinands (2012)	71	15	3	9	1
Men and Women Religious					
Men and women in perpetual vows	94%	3%	1%	2%	<1%
Women professing perpetual vows (2011)	66	10	4	17	3
Men professing perpetual vows (2011)*	50	0	12	38	0
Lay Persons					
Lay ecclesial ministers	88%	9%	2%	1%	<1%
Adult Mass-attending Catholics (inv-pew)	62	26	2	5	5
All adult Catholics	58	35	3	3	1

*Estimates for new religious brothers are based on a small sample.

Sources: The CARA Catholic Poll; CARA Pastoral Assistance Surveys and Services; In-Pew Cumulative Statistics; Gray et al. 2011; Gautier and O'Hara 2011; Bendyna and Gautier 2009; Gautier and Gray 2012; Gautier et al. 2012; Gautier and Gaunt 2015.

Catholic population.[2] Much of the racial and ethnic diversity of the U.S. Catholic population is concentrated among those born after 1960. As more of these younger Catholics enter ministry roles, the diversity of lay ecclesial ministers is likely to increase. This is best represented in the diversity among those enrolled in lay ecclesial ministry formation programs today.[3]

CONCLUSION

The parish of today has evolved into a community where there is increasing co-responsibility for ministry between clergy and lay people. In 2010 CARA estimated the total number of people on Catholic parish staffs in the United States was 168,448. This included both ordained and lay ministry staff and volunteers as well as nonministry staff and volunteers (parish bookkeepers, groundskeepers, cooks, etc.). The average parish had a total staff size of 9.5, with 5.4 individuals in ministry positions. The estimated number of lay ecclesial ministers (defined empirically as those paid in ministry for at least 20 hours per week) at that time was approximately 38,000. This represents 23 percent of all parish staff and 40 percent of all staff members involved in ministry. CARA estimates that the Catholic Church in the United States in recent years has increased by about 430 lay ecclesial ministers on parish ministry staffs each year, for a total of about 40,000 in the United States at the end of 2014.[4]

To put this population of lay ecclesial ministers in context, we calculated estimates for a variety of different Catholic subgroups

2. Data for this table were compiled from other CARA research and first presented in Gray and Gautier 2012.

3. Hispanics/Latino(a)s make up almost half (47 percent) of participants in lay ecclesial ministry formation programs. White/Anglo/Caucasian participants make up a little more than 44 percent. Blacks/African Americans and Asians/Pacific Islanders make up another 3 percent each. Others (including Native Americans) also make up 3 percent of enrollees in these programs (Gautier et al. 2015).

4. This estimate represents *net* additions—accounting for lay ecclesial ministers who retire, pass away, or leave ministry for some other reason.

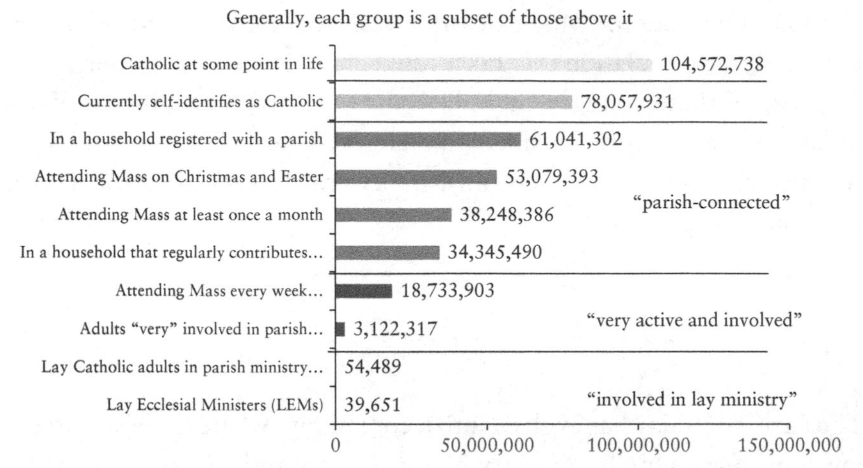

Figure 3.10 U.S. Catholic Populations and Parish Life, 2014.
Source: Gray 2015a.

in Figure 3.10. More than 100 million people in the United States in 2014 are baptized Catholics, and more than 78 million of them self-identify as Catholic. Far fewer were very active in the life and community of a parish or served in a parish leadership role. About 18.7 million attend Mass on a weekly basis (i.e., at least once a week *every* week). Significantly fewer, about 3.1 million, report that they are "very" involved in their parish beyond attending Mass. More than 54,000 are involved in pastoral ministry in their parish, and not quite 40,000 are lay ecclesial ministers. So although lay ecclesial ministers are still just a very small subset of all Catholics, their contribution to parish pastoral ministry is outsized and growing.

The next chapter examines in some detail the variety of parish reconfiguration strategies that dioceses have implemented to cope with changes in population demographics over the past quarter-century.

CHAPTER FOUR

PARISH RECONFIGURATION STRATEGIES

Who is minding the local American Catholic parish? As we saw in chapter 3, the answer to that question has been gradually changing in recent decades. The number of diocesan priests has been declining, from more than 34,000 in 1990 to just under 26,000 in 2014. At the same time new lay professional staff have been added to help meet pastoral ministry needs.

As Figure 4.1 shows, the estimated number of lay ecclesial ministers serving in U.S. parishes surpassed the total number of diocesan priests in the early 2000s. Currently there are about 40,000 of these individuals providing ministry in parishes in the United States.

Yet to have Mass and celebrate sacraments every parish still needs priests. Nationally there were 16,462 active diocesan priests and 17,324 parishes in 2014.[1] The last time the number of these clergy was larger than the number of parishes in the United States was 2004. Some priests who are members of religious orders (such as Jesuits and Franciscans) also serve as pastors, and significant numbers of international priests have come to the United States to minister in parishes in recent decades, as we saw in chapter 3. Retired priests often help out as well.

1. Out of a total diocesan presbyteral workforce of 25,868 in 2014, *The Official Catholic Directory* reports that 36 percent of these men are either retired, inactive for health reasons, or on a leave of absence for some other reason and therefore not available for parish ministry.

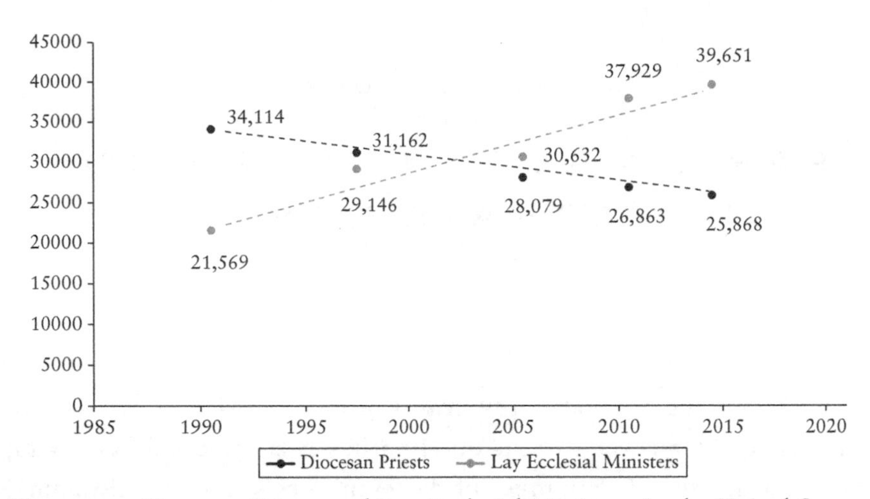

Figure 4.1 Diocesan Priests and Lay Ecclesial Ministers in the United States, 1990–2014.

Sources: The Official Catholic Directory, relevant years (priest data); CARA National Survey of Catholic Parishes 2014; DeLambo 2005; Gray et al. 2011; Murnion 1992; Murnion and DeLambo 1999 (lay ecclesial minister data).

One option available to bishops who are coping with fewer priests than parishes in their diocese is to assign a single pastor responsibility for multiple parishes (canon 526.1). Dioceses employ different names for this process, such as clustering, linking, and twinning parishes. Each parish retains its own canonical identity, including its own pastoral and finance councils, although they might also establish interparochial councils to address common parish issues. Each parish might also retain its own staff, although typically there is some sharing of staff.

Another option is for a team of priests to be assigned shared responsibility for several parishes (canon 517.1), such as three priests pastoring five parishes. Each priest in the team has the obligations and responsibilities of a pastor in each parish. The bishop appoints one of the priests to serve as team moderator to coordinate the group's activities.

When no priest is available, bishops can utilize canon 517.2 and entrust the pastoral care of a parish to a permanent deacon, a religious sister or brother, or a lay person, most typically referred to as a parish life coordinator (PLC). The PLC is not the pastor; the bishop or his delegate serves as the canonical pastor of the parish. A priest (who may or may not be the canonical pastor) is assigned by the bishop to provide a sacramental presence. The PLC manages the daily operations of the parish, oversees sacramental preparation and other ministry duties, and presides at services in the absence of a priest on weekends when the sacramental priest is not available. At these services communion hosts that have been consecrated previously by a priest may be distributed.

Another option is to merge parishes, creating a brand new parish from the territory of two or more existing parishes. Alternatively one parish is closed and its territory is consolidated with an existing parish.

The total number of parishes in the United States in 2014 is very similar to what it was in 1965. In 1988 the number of parishes peaked at 19,705. Since then the Church has merged or consolidated more parishes than it has created new parishes, for a net decline of 2,368 parishes (–12 percent). In spite of a popular misconception, when a parish is consolidated or merged the amalgamated parish, not the diocese, takes possession of all the affected parishes' assets and liabilities.

PRIEST SHORTAGES AND PARISH CONFIGURATIONS

Which dioceses have the greatest mismatch between active diocesan priests and parishes? In 2014 nine of the top 10 were in the Midwest, as shown in Table 4.1. For example, the Diocese of Green Bay, Wisconsin, reported 64 active diocesan priests and 157 parishes in the 2015 *Official Catholic Directory*. In all, 81 parishes in that diocese were without a resident pastor. Forty-five of the diocese's parishes had a nonresident priest pastor, and in 36 parishes the pastoral care of the parish was entrusted to a deacon or lay person (canon 517.2). Nineteen of these parishes were entrusted to deacons, 10 to religious sisters, and seven to other lay persons.

Why would so many midwestern dioceses have fewer active diocesan priests than parishes? As we described in chapter 2, this region of the country used to be a population center for U.S. Catholicism. However, as the transformation of the U.S. labor market from an industrial to a postindustrial economy took place during the 20th

Table 4.1 U.S. Dioceses with More Parishes than Active Diocesan Priests

	Active Diocesan Priests	Parishes	Difference	Parishes without Resident Pastor	Canon 517.2 Parishes
1. Green Bay, WI	64	157	−93	81	36
2. La Crosse, WI	78	160	−82	55	0
3. Dubuque, IA	88	166	−78	97	14
4. St. Cloud, MN	56	131	−75	71	0
5. Superior, WI	31	103	−72	69	21
6. Richmond, VA	82	143	−61	40	0
7. Rapid City, SD	26	84	−58	56	0
7. Springfield, IL	71	129	−58	73	4
7. Winona, MN	56	114	−58	64	0
10. Sioux City, IA	54	111	−57	63	0

Source: *The Official Catholic Directory* 2015.

century and parts of this region became known as the Rust Belt, many Catholics (along with other Americans) moved to areas in the South and the West, the Sun Belt, where the jobs were. In other words, the Catholics moved, but the parishes remained. These Rust Belt dioceses still serve a sizable Catholic population, but it is aging. Many young adults who were raised in the region ended up migrating elsewhere.

Geography is important in other ways as well. In rural America it can be difficult to implement a multiparish ministry, the configuration in which a single pastor (sometimes with other pastoral ministers) serves in multiple parishes. In urban areas in which parishes are in close proximity, a priest may be able to function well as a resident pastor in one parish and a nonresident pastor in another. When parishes are separated by many miles, however, this model becomes more challenging. Bishops may also be reluctant to close a parish located in a rural area if the parish serves a community whose members may not easily travel to the next nearest parish. In some dioceses bishops appoint PLCs to keep parishes open when they do not have enough priests to staff them all.

PARISH LIFE COORDINATORS

Nationally, according to the 2015 edition of *The Official Catholic Directory*, there are 369 parishes entrusted to PLCs under canon 517.2.[2] The number of parishes entrusted to deacons or lay persons peaked at 566 in 2004. There are more priests retiring or passing away each year than there are new ordinations. This decline in the number of active diocesan priests is expected to continue for some time, as is the net decline in the number of parishes each year. These two trends are not unrelated.

There were 3,448 U.S. parishes without a resident pastor in 2014. Most, 89 percent, were administered by nonresident pastors. Just 4 percent of parishes without a resident pastor were entrusted to a deacon, 3 percent to lay men or women, and 2 percent to a religious sister. Fewer than 1 percent were entrusted to a religious brother or to a configuration known as a "pastoral team," which in most cases means several priests jointly pastoring several parishes. When the 2015 *Official Catholic Directory* data were collected a total of eight parishes remained vacant, meaning the diocese had not yet appointed a pastor or a PLC.

The appointment of a PLC is an option available to a bishop when a diocese is faced with a shortage of priests. Some bishops entrust parishes to deacons and other lay persons; others use nonresident priest pastors; and some choose to close parishes where they can. The dioceses of Green Bay, Wisconsin, Superior, Wisconsin, and Albany, New York, each have more than 10 parishes in which the pastoral care of the parish is entrusted to deacons. The Diocese of Green Bay also has ten parishes entrusted to religious sisters. Fairbanks, Alaska, has 15 parishes entrusted to lay men and women. Albany has nine parishes entrusted to lay people, and Green Bay and Jackson, Mississippi, have seven parishes each entrusted as such. In La Crosse, Wisconsin, Richmond,

2. The parish administration data for a number of dioceses do not balance in *The Official Catholic Directory*. The analysis here includes corrections to the reported data to be as accurate as possible.

Virginia, Winona, Minnesota, and other dioceses there are numerous parishes without resident pastors but no canon 517.2 parishes.

The examination by the Center for Applied Research into the Apostolate (CARA) of the PLC data reported in *The Official Catholic Directory* shows that one of the best indicators of the number of PLCs in a diocese is the figure created by subtracting the number of parishes from the number of active diocesan priests.[3] When this number is positive and there is a "surplus" of active diocesan priests as compared to parishes, the likelihood that a PLC is appointed is lowest.[4] When this number is negative, indicating more parishes than active diocesan priests, the likelihood that there is at least one PLC appointed increases. The greater the disparity between parishes and active diocesan priests, the greater the likelihood that PLCs will be appointed.

In the absence of a sufficient number of active diocesan priests a bishop may assign priests brought in from outside of the diocese (i.e., extern priests) to fulfill pastoral needs. Analysis of the data reveals that predicting the number of PLCs in a diocese is strengthened when the number of extern priests is considered. Thus there is an even greater likelihood that PLCs will be entrusted with parishes in a diocese where the total number of parishes exceeds the combined number of active diocesan priests and extern priests. The data also reveal the importance of a second structural factor in addition to the number of priests: PLCs are more likely to be appointed by bishops in dioceses where the number of parishes is greater than the number of priests *and* where the number of square miles per parish is comparatively high. This factor is representative of the average distances a nonresident priest pastor would need to travel between multiple parishes to provide for their sacramental needs. When this number

3. Analyses of the data reveal that the number of religious priests in a diocese is empirically less important in explaining the appointments of PLCs. The number of retired priests is also shown to be of much lesser importance. Although the presence of both of these types of priests may represent options for a bishop, it appears that many of these priests are unavailable to fill the role of pastor, whether due to other roles and obligations they have or, in the case of retired priests, poor health.

4. The "surplus" is theoretical. In reality many parishes have sufficient pastoral needs to warrant more than one priest per parish.

is large (in excess of approximately 90 square miles per parish) and the number of parishes exceeds the number of active diocesan and extern priests, there is an even greater likelihood that a bishop will appoint PLCs.

Another option for dealing with fewer priests relative to the number of parishes is to reorganize parishes through closings and mergers. However, the data reveal that this type of decision is impacted by one final structural factor: the number of Catholics per parish. In some dioceses where the Catholic population is declining or stagnant this is an option that bishops have selected. However, this option appears more difficult to implement in dioceses where the Catholic population is growing. Where the Catholic population is growing and the number of parishes is not, and where the number of parishes exceeds the number of active diocesan priests, the likelihood that PLCs will be appointed is even more likely.

Although each of these factors is an important indicator of when a bishop may decide to appoint a PLC, together they cannot explain *most* of the differences between dioceses or within a diocese over time.[5] CARA's analyses of the data indicate that perhaps the most important factor is noted in the first words of canon 517.2: "If the diocesan bishop should decide." Beyond the structural pressures (the number of parishes, priests, and Catholics, as well as the size of the diocese) the particular bishop making the decision is the most important indicator of whether and how many PLCs will be appointed in a diocese.

BISHOPS AND PARISH LIFE COORDINATORS

In 2005 CARA conducted focus groups with Catholic bishops to explore their decision making regarding canon 517.2 parishes as part

5. Regression analysis of the data indicates that the structural factors explain 23 percent of the variation in the number of PLCs between dioceses and within a diocese over time. Thus most of the differences in the number of PLCs across dioceses and across time are attributable to factors other than these structural pressures.

of the Emerging Models of Pastoral Leadership Project (Gautier et al. 2007). A total of 45 bishops were interviewed for this project. Overall these bishops reported a positive assessment of their experience with PLCs. Most, however, identified PLCs as a less than ideal solution to the priest shortage, better considered a temporary measure until priests can be assigned as pastors. On the other hand, bishops described generally positive reactions among parishioners to bringing in a PLC. Some say that PLCs bring new life to parishes and new perspectives on ministry. A few bishops admit their own surprise at how well-received these PLCs are in the parishes to which they are assigned. There are also tensions, however, including fear among parishioners that the assignment of a PLC means the parish will soon be closed by the bishop. Other tensions revolve around questions regarding the proper role of lay persons in ministry.

Participating bishops described some tension between PLCs and canonical pastors, along with the potential for blurring lines between the ordained and nonordained. Conflicts may arise over who is responsible for preaching and pastoral care. Bishops said they must take care to explain to PLCs that their role is temporary and that they must be prepared for the possibility of being replaced by a priest should one become available.

Here is a representative sample of what the bishops told CARA researchers about their experience assigning PLCs:

- My general experience is a very positive one.
- Well, we've had situations where the sisters have left and lay people have come in. The parish council says, "We want another one of those lay people who can say Mass," and they request a parish director rather than a priest.
- The deacons are very good, very qualified. A couple people now who are pastoral coordinators or whatever have more business sense. So they've got a lot of experience before they take the job of deacon. And they're very, very cooperative.
- I don't think, from what I've heard from other places, that there's a lot of positive outputs from [using PLCs]. That doesn't say that

there are or there aren't. They may be.... Formation of the laity is what's lacking.... We're confusing who's ordained, who's not ordained, what the proper roles are. So I would be very cautious in anything we would do until we really have a laity that's educated and understand their life and their major role in the Church.

- My personal approach to [assigning PLCs] has never been that it was the ideal situation.
- Some [PLCs] that I've seen have been excellent, and some have caused a lot of problems. The ones who have been excellent, though, really did have this heart and soul [of the] Church; they were the ones to take the lead in praying for vocations and in promoting vocations to the priesthood. But I would need to see that in someone to whom I would entrust [a parish].
- I think some of us are in a position where we have no choice; we have to [assign PLCs].
- The ideal would [be to] have a good priest. But [if] there is a choice between having a local parish life coordinator [or] a foreign priest, especially one who comes from overseas, then I would say it might be a toss-up.

MISMATCH BETWEEN POPULATION AND PARISHES

Bishops must balance the number of available priests with the needs of the Catholic population. They often do this while also evaluating the changing demographics of their diocese. As we described in chapter 2, the share of the Catholic population residing in the Northeast and Midwest has been in decline since the 1970s. The Catholic population is now more evenly divided among regions. In the coming decades, if current trends continue, it will become more and more a "southern" Church.

As these population shifts have occurred, the Catholic Church's U.S. parishes, many built to serve urban immigrants of the distant past, have become misaligned with the 21st-century Catholic population (see Figure 4.2). The bricks-and-mortar version of the Church is slow to move.

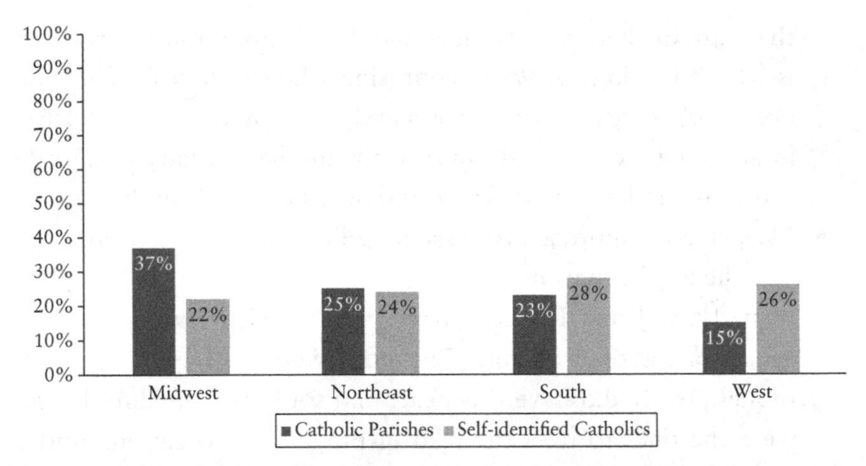

Figure 4.2 Distribution of Parishes and Population in the United States, 2014.
Sources: CARA National Survey of Catholic Parishes 2014 (self-identified Catholics); *The Official Catholic Directory*. 2015 (parishes).

The Midwest has 37 percent of parishes and just 22 percent of the self-identified Catholic population. By comparison the West has only 15 percent of parishes and 26 percent of the Catholic population (as of 2014). The Church is managing to close parishes where they are not viable but is lagging a bit in building new parishes where they are needed most.

The dioceses losing Catholic population in the largest numbers in the past decade include Brooklyn (–275,600), Detroit (–237,000), Pittsburgh (–167,900), and Chicago (–157,000). The fastest growing are Galveston-Houston (+667,600), Atlanta (+633,000), Fresno (+619,000), and Phoenix (+589,900).

CARA's surveys of pastors and PLCs for the Emerging Models Study allow us to create profiles of parishes with different staffing configurations, including PLC or canon 517.2 parishes as well as those parishes using the multiparish ministry approach, often without resident priest pastors.

PROFILES OF RECONFIGURATION

More than a quarter of PLC parishes (27 percent) were established before 1875. Many of these older parishes are in urban areas of the

Northeast and Midwest. In terms of the year of construction of church buildings, PLC parishes are similar to all parishes in the United States. PLC parishes, however, are much more likely than other parishes nationally to have a small seating capacity (47 percent have fewer than 270 seats). The average seating capacity in a PLC parish is 296. The average number of Mass attenders on a typical weekend in October in PLC parishes is 352. This number of attenders represents 53 percent of the number of registered individuals in a PLC parish, on average, and 47 percent of the church's capacity (i.e., seats multiplied by number of Masses). The median number of weekend Masses celebrated in PLC parishes is two, compared to four in U.S. parishes overall. Forty-one percent of PLC parishes celebrate only one Mass each weekend. Thirty-six percent of PLC parishes do not have any weekday Masses.

PLC parishes celebrate fewer Masses than other parishes but also rarely hold any Sunday Celebrations in the Absence of a Priest. Only about a third (35 percent) of parishes entrusted to a PLC report at least one of these celebrations in a year. Among those that do, most indicate celebrating fewer than 10 a year.

Multiparish ministry (MPM) parishes are also concentrated in the Midwest (57 percent) and Northeast (22 percent). They tend to be smaller than the typical U.S. parish, with an average of 566 registered households and a seating capacity of 393. MPM parishes, on average, have 499 attenders at all Saturday Vigil and Sunday Masses in October. This typically represents 44 percent of registered individuals and 50 percent of the parish capacity.

CARA surveyed parish staffs in parishes that had recently been affected by a reorganization, such as a merger, a closing, or the creation of a new parish (Figure 4.3). These leaders were most likely to say that the unhappiness of parishioners (50 percent) and finding enough volunteers (43 percent) were at least "somewhat" difficult for them. Parish leaders were less likely to indicate the following as being at least "somewhat" difficult since reorganization: coordination of time between parishes (34 percent), interaction of staff members from parishes (26 percent), and getting support from their archdiocese or diocese (25 percent).

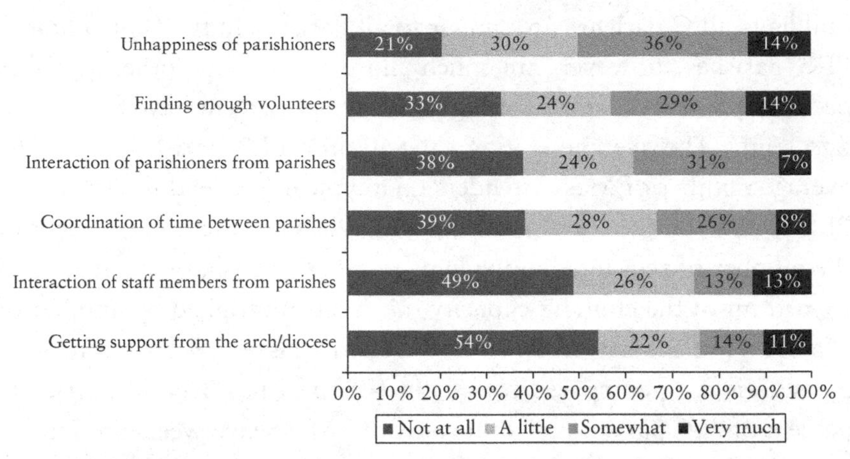

Figure 4.3 Difficulties since Reorganization.

Source: Gray 2012.

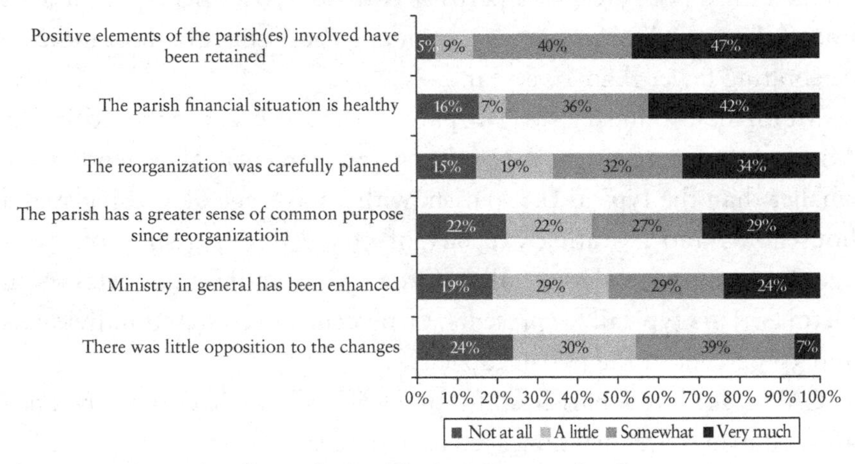

Figure 4.4 Attitudes about the Parish since Reorganization.

Source: Gray 2012.

Responding to a second set of questions (see Figure 4.4), most leaders in parishes affected by reorganization agree "somewhat" or "very much" that the positive elements of the parishes involved were retained (87 percent); 78 percent agree at least "somewhat" that their parish's financial situation is healthy; and 66 percent agree "somewhat" or

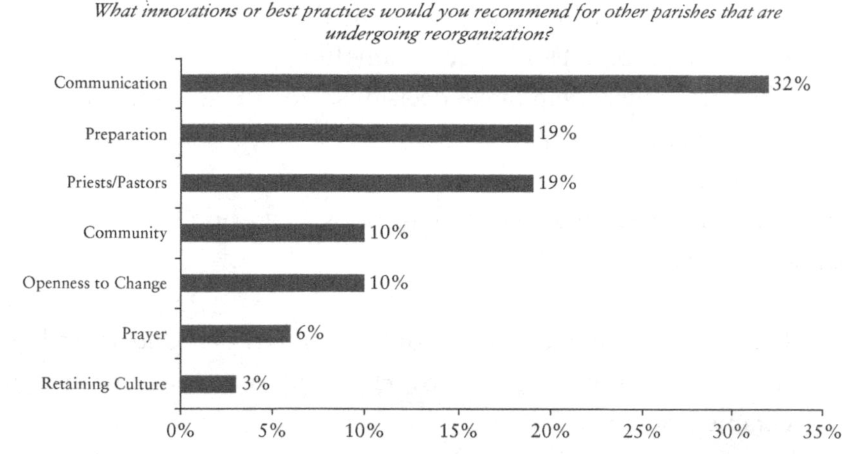

Figure 4.5 Innovations or Best Practices for Parishes Undergoing Reorganization.
Source: Gray 2012.

"very much" that the reorganization they experienced was carefully planned. Parish leaders were more divided in their agreement with other issues: 56 percent agree at least "somewhat" that their parish has a greater sense of common purpose since the reorganization; 53 percent responded similarly when asked if ministry in general has been enhanced. A minority (46 percent) agree at least "somewhat" that there was little opposition to the changes in their parish.

We also asked the leaders in recently reorganized parishes about any innovations or best practices they would recommend for other parishes undergoing reorganization. Responses were recoded into categories and are displayed by the frequency of each type of comment made by respondents in Figure 4.5.[6] A third of comments from these parish leaders (32 percent) emphasized the need for communication. This was the most common type of response. Examples follow:

- Communication, training, spiritual enhancement, and involvement.
- Frequent and detailed information be given to members of the parishes.

6. Responses can include multiple ideas and therefore more than one coded comment.

- Keep the parish members apprised of all communication and status of the process. Don't assume anything.
- The parishioners help make decisions. Don't command. Have all groups meet together.

Nineteen percent emphasized preparations that should be made or issues of timing:

- Preparation of any kind for people, staff, pastors. Understanding that all will not go perfectly. Hire staff that are capable of communication.
- Six months is an adequate time frame.
- Prepare. If possible, share the rationale of your decision. Be open.
- Training helpful.

About 19 percent referenced issues with priests or their pastors:

- A reorganization requires more priests. One priest cannot manage two parishes without making sacrifices of himself and of parishioners.
- Don't take away the number of priests when you join two parishes. We went from 2 to 1.
- Let your parish pastor be the leader. He has the best ideas.
- More care taken on assignment of priests to multipastoral congregations, Consider demographics.

Ten percent or fewer emphasized issues of community, openness to change, prayer, or the need to retain existing parish cultures:

- Be open to change and consolidation.
- For both parishes this is not easy. Some parishioners do not feel comfortable going to another church. Parishioners were not happy not having an office at [parish name].
- I know it is difficult to close parishes—but it is my opinion that keeping parishes open puts more importance on the building than the community.

- Keep praying.
- Parish leaders need to avoid the perception of a hidden agenda.
- Take your time. Involve as many people as possible.
- Provide a workshop/forum etc. for parishioners to express/answer concerns.
- Let each parish retain its own culture and tradition.

CATHOLICS' ATTITUDES ABOUT RECONFIGURATION

In CARA's 2008 national survey of adult self-identified Catholics, we asked respondents what they would prefer for their parish if a priest was no longer available. Overall 55 percent said they would "support" or "strongly support" "increasing the use of lay ecclesial ministers. As shown in Table 4.2, self-identified Catholics who attend Mass weekly or

Table 4.2 Support for Parish Staffing Alternatives

Percentage of parishioners who "support" or "strongly support" each:			
	By Mass Attendance		
	Weekly or More	Less than Weekly but at Least Once a Month	A Few Times a Year or Less
Sharing a priest with one or more other parishes	76%	78%	56%
Bringing in a priest from outside of the United States	73	67	45
Asking a retired priest to come in and do more	71	59	46
Increasing the use of deacons	68	70	46
Increasing the use of lay ecclesial ministers	60	56	38
Merging the parish with another nearby parish	50	51	40

Source: Gray and Perl 2008.

more often (i.e., those most likely to be in the pews) even more strongly support the increased use of lay ecclesial ministers (60 percent).

However, it is also important to note that there are several other alternatives (including some that involve parish reconfiguration) that have broader support among the most frequent attenders, including sharing a priest with another parish (76 percent), bringing in a priest from outside the United States (73 percent), asking a retired priest to come in and do more (71 percent), and increasing the use of deacons (68 percent). The least favored option is merging the parish with a nearby parish (50 percent).

CONCLUSION

Parish reconfigurations were under way at the time of the Notre Dame Study, although the net number of parishes across the United States continued to increase until the mid-1990s. Those early reconfigurations took place primarily in the Midwest and more rural parts of the Northeast. Since that time many midwestern dioceses have felt the need to conduct a second and even third round of reconfigurations, and East Coast dioceses have begun to catch up and conduct reconfigurations on a larger scale.

As a result neighborhood parishes with several priests and religious sisters at the ready to serve the needs of the community are for the most part gone in the United States. Parishioners are traveling farther to attend Mass and celebrate sacraments in larger communities. Sometimes there is no priest in the parish, and sisters are an even rarer sight. More often the first parish staff member one might see and talk to is another lay person or perhaps a deacon.

The Catholic Church has adapted and continues to adapt to its shifting demographic realities. Increasingly it is becoming a "tale of two Churches." Some bishops in the Northeast and Midwest are inviting more international priests; others are entrusting parishes to deacons or lay people; and still others are closing and merging parishes where possible in the face of a declining Catholic population. In the South and

West bishops are struggling to build new parishes and infrastructure to serve the needs of a rapidly growing population. Here and elsewhere in merged or MPM parishes large staffs with many lay ecclesial ministers are needed to serve the needs of a growing community.

The Catholic Church has weathered many challenges in the past. In some ways the Church in the United States is simply undergoing an identity change. The neighborhood parish is being transformed into the regional community parish, a site that relies on the collaboration and co-responsibility of available clergy, vowed religious, and lay people. In the next chapter we examine changes in the administration of these increasingly complex parishes.

CHAPTER FIVE

PARISH ADMINISTRATION

Although the Notre Dame Study virtually ignored parish administration issues, administration has taken on an increasing amount of scrutiny in the years since that study was completed. While very few parishes consider themselves wealthy in terms of their finances, most parishes must deal with limited or sometimes dwindling resources while providing an expanding amount of services to a growing Catholic population. Many parishes are saddled with old facilities that need regular repair and maintenance. The decline in religious vocations has meant that most parish staff members are laity, typically with advanced education and/or experience, who expect and deserve to be paid a competitive salary. Because of parish mergers and other organizational reconfigurations, as described in chapter 4, a growing number of priests are being asked to pastor larger parishes or multiple parishes. On top of this, stories of embezzlement by parish employees (both lay and clergy) have scandalized the faithful. All of this calls for a heightened focus on parish administration.

The pastor is the chief executive officer of the parish. Canon 519 states that the pastor is to carry out the threefold functions of teaching, sanctifying, and governing. Saint Paul, in 1 Corinthians 12:27–31, tells us that administration is a charism. Pastors need to be familiar with a wide range of issues, including those having to do with finances, human resources, and the physical plant. While most seminaries do an excellent job of preparing men for their teaching and sanctifying roles, they do less to prepare these men for their governing role. The curriculum is focused on preparing priests, but not necessarily pastors.

Even at the time of the Notre Dame Study it wasn't as important for seminaries to prepare their graduates for administrative tasks. Once ordained, priests could expect to spend several years as parochial vicars (assistant pastors), learning about all aspects of parish life, including the governing function. However, with the decline in the number of priests, the newly ordained now are often named pastors one or two years after ordination. They miss out on the benefits of being mentored that earlier generations of priests had received.

All of this is compounded by the fact that many pastors are charged with administering larger and in some cases multiple parishes. In order to succeed, pastors need to rely more heavily on laity to perform many administrative tasks in the parish. Some of the lay staff have a background in the business world (although most do not). But even those who do have a business background usually lack an understanding of how a parish operates (e.g., reliance on volunteers and donations).

In assessing the current state of pastoral administration, it is helpful to employ the construct used to analyze management in the business world, which identifies four management functions: planning, organizing, leading, and controlling.

FUNCTIONS OF PARISH MANAGEMENT

PLANNING

The parish planning function entails developing mission and vision statements along with goals and objectives. A mission statement answers the question "Why does the parish exist?" A vision statement answers the question "What will the future look like as the parish fulfills its mission? What will be different?" While mission is about today, vision is about the future, what the parish will become. Once a parish has developed its mission and vision it can begin working toward them by establishing goals and objectives. Goals are broad, primary outcomes, while objectives are measureable steps taken to achieve a goal. Since objectives are to be measureable, part of the planning process involves developing metrics to quantify parish activities. The two most common types of parish metrics are counting participants (at Mass, at speakers, at social events, etc.) and surveying parishioners.

Data on individual parish mission statements are not available. However, one of the surveys that was part of the Emerging Models Study asked parishioners about the vision provided by the pastor or PLC as well as the vision provided by the overall parish leadership. Parishioners in traditional parishes (with a resident priest pastor) were most likely and parishioners in consolidated parishes were least likely to rate highly the vision provided by the pastor. The vision provided by parish leadership overall (including the pastor and other parish leaders) was rated highest in traditional and MPM parishes and lowest in consolidated and PLC parishes. The fact that the more stable traditional parishes had the highest rating for both groups should not come as a surprise.

The research also shows some disappointing results when it comes to deriving parish metrics to support the planning process. Only about two-thirds of the parishes responding to the National Survey of Catholic Parishes bothered to count parish Mass attenders or participants at parish functions, and fewer than 50 percent made the effort to survey parishioners. Almost one in five made no effort to measure the impact of their programs. Parishes that fail to gather metrics on their programs are unable to answer critical questions such as these:

- How will we know when we are accomplishing our mission?
- How will we know that we have impacted our parishioners?
- How will we know how effective the church staff is?
- How will we know if our programs are effective?
- How will we know how to allocate our financial resources?

Without the answers to these questions such parishes are unable to plan effectively.

ORGANIZING

The management function of organizing involves developing an organizational structure and allocating human resources to ensure the accomplishment of goals and objectives. Organizing also involves the design of individual jobs within the organization. The duties and responsibilities of individual positions, as well as the manner in which the duties should be carried out, need to be determined.

The chain of command within an organization can be represented graphically in an organization reporting chart. Fr. Thomas Sweetser SJ, a highly regarded parish consultant, has long argued for a revision of the typical Catholic parish reporting chart. In most parishes, Fr. Sweetser (2001) has observed, the chart can be illustrated by a circle, with the pastor as the circle's focus. The entire staff reports directly to the pastor, and all decisions flow through him. A better system, he argues, is represented by an ellipse, which has two focal points, or foci. In his system these foci represent a pastor and a parish administrator. The two work closely together, but each maintains their own responsibilities: the pastor has primary responsibility for the pastoral tasks of the parish, while the parish administrator is responsible for the temporal or business side of running a parish. This type of relationship is observed frequently in our society, in the form of a chief executive officer and a chief operating officer in a corporation.

The successful implementation of this system requires two critical elements:

1. The two need to agree on which aspects of parish life **must** be overseen by the pastor, which tasks require ordination and which do not. Those that do not can be placed under the administrative responsibilities of the parish administrator. These include all of the financial, personnel, and facilities matters.
2. The parish needs to find a professionally qualified parish administrator. In many parishes the closest thing to a parish administrator is the parish business manager. Many business managers are retired from business and are not experienced in issues facing faith-based organizations, such as dealing with volunteers and relying on contributions as the primary source of revenue. Many prefer to work only part time. Other parishes employ business managers who have a limited business background and whose primary qualification is that they are active parishioners. In order

> for the elliptical model to be effective, it is imperative that the parish administrator is as professionally qualified to manage the temporal side of the parish as the pastor is to conduct the pastoral sphere.

A related issue is the need to educate parishioners and staff, who are accustomed to approaching the pastor on all parish matters, on the necessity of recognizing the parish administrator's authority over temporal matters.

The elliptical model has the obvious benefit of helping to alleviate the clergy shortage by reducing the burden on priests as parishes get larger and as some are merged and others are closed. This parish organizational structure would be particularly beneficial in situations where one priest is pastoring multiple parishes. Another benefit of this model is that it relieves the pastor of many tasks for which most have not received any prior education or training.

A downside of this model is that it can be costly for a parish to pay the compensation required to attract and retain professionally qualified parish administrators. This would be especially burdensome on some smaller parishes. For those parishes it would make sense to arrange to share a parish administrator.

The National Survey of Catholic Parishes asked questions concerning the organizational reporting structure for paid parish staff who are involved in ministry (such as the director of religious education and the music minister) and the paid nonministry staff (such as custodians and secretaries) Under Fr. Sweetser's system best practices would have ministry staff reporting to the pastor and nonministry staff reporting to another individual, such as a parish business manager or pastoral associate. While one could make the case for ministry staff reporting to the pastor, there is less reason for the pastor to have responsibility for nonministry staff reporting to him.

Fewer than three in ten parishes employ a parish business manager (28 percent), but of those that do, a large majority (79 percent) are employed full time.Figure 5.1 displays the proportion within each parish organizational structure that employ a parish business manager.

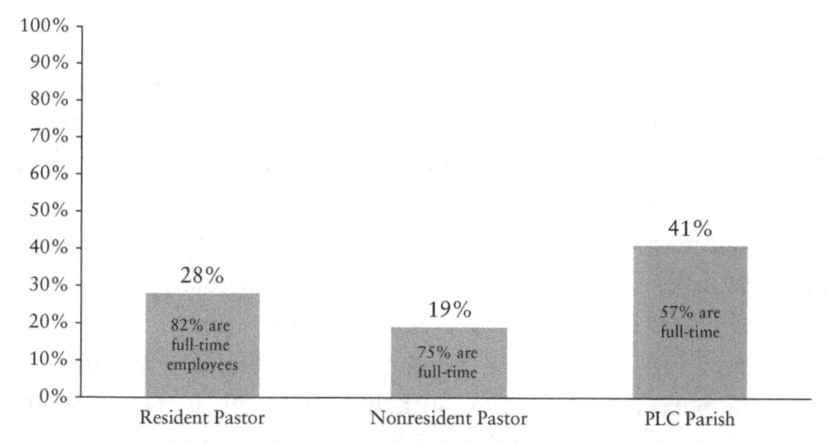

Figure 5.1 Parishes Employing a Business Manager or Administrator by Parish Staffing Structure.

Source: CARA National Survey of Catholic Parishes 2014.

PLC parishes are the most likely to employ a business manager but the least likely to employ one full time.

Fr. Sweetser's system would have priests overseeing ministry staff (such as the director of religious education), while a parish business manager oversees nonministry staff (such as the parish custodian). However, the data show that in parishes staffed by resident pastors as well as those staffed by nonresident pastors, 92 percent oversee ministry personnel, and a large majority (69 percent and 73 percent, respectively) oversee nonministry parish personnel as well. By contrast, in 75 percent of PLC parishes the PLC oversees the ministry personnel, and in 62 percent of PLC parishes they oversee the parish nonministry personnel.

As parishes become larger and more complex, many have hired professionally trained staff in key positions. At the same time the priest shortage is placing a greater strain on priests who are called to pastor these larger parishes or multiple parishes. Changing the parish organizational reporting chart from a circle, with the pastor as the focus, to an ellipse, with the pastor and a parish business manager dividing the management tasks, is not only more efficient but also places less of a burden on the dwindling number of priests available to serve as pastors.

LEADING

Leading entails influencing others toward the attainment of organizational goals. Effective parish leadership requires the pastor to motivate staff and parishioners, communicate with them, and effectively use informal power, based on relationship building rather than exerting authority. Successful leadership results in parish staff and parishioners enthusiastically working together to attain parish goals.

Specific leadership activities include motivating, training, and communicating. The Parish Leaders Survey asked respondents to rate their parish on its success in achieving each of these activities. As seen in Figure 5.2, parish leaders see themselves as successful in encouraging parishioners to participate, but much less successful in giving them a role in decision making. Likewise they consider themselves more successful in communicating with parishioners and promoting ministry opportunities than listening to parishioners' input or concerns.

The Emerging Models Study asked parishioners a battery of questions about motivation and communication from their perspective. Figure 5.3 shows that parishioners are less likely than parish leaders to feel encouraged to participate in parish ministry. Fewer than half of

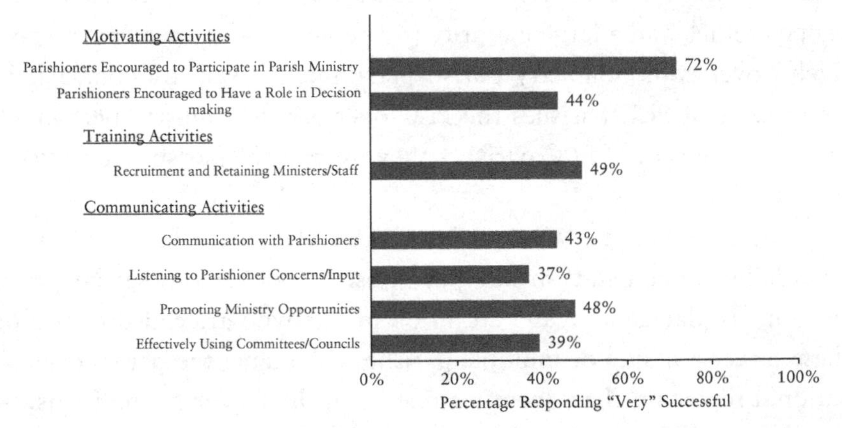

Figure 5.2 Parish Leaders' Self-Evaluation of Success in Motivating, Training, and Communicating.

Source: Gray 2012.

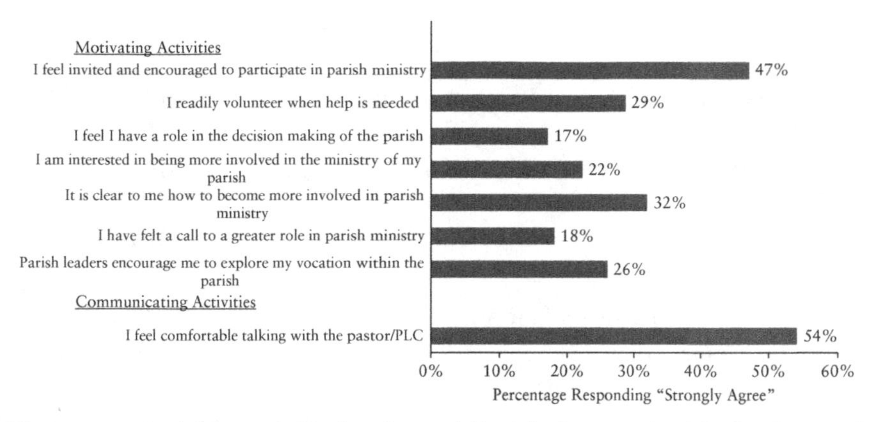

Figure 5.3 Parishioners' Evaluation of Parish Success in Motivating and Communicating.

Source: Gray et al. 2013.

parishioners "strongly agree" that they feel invited and encouraged to participate in parish ministry. Similarly parishioners are less likely to feel they have a role in parish decision making. Parishioners rate their parishes highest for their efforts to encourage parishioners to participate in parish ministries and for being clear on what steps parishioners should take to become involved. At the same time many parishioners have not felt a call to become more active in ministries. More than half feel comfortable talking with their pastor or PLC, but that apparently did not translate into a sense that they had a role in parish decision making.

CONTROLLING

Controlling involves ensuring that performance does not deviate from standards. It compares where the parish actually is to where parish leadership wants it to be, and then responding. Controlling consists of three steps: (1) establishing performance standards, (2) comparing actual performance against standards, and (3) taking corrective action when necessary.

Recall that rather than having the pastor supervise all parish staff, Fr. Sweetser proposes a two-headed arrangement: all ministry staff would report to the pastor, and nonministry staff would report to a

Table 5.1 Ministry Staff Performance Appraisal

Ministry staff received formal performance appraisal	48%
Compensation affected by appraisal	44%
Received appraisal from:	
Pastor/priest	81%
517.2 administrator	3%
Parish manager/administrator	8%
Combination	6%
Other	1%

Source: CARA National Survey of Catholic Parishes 2014.

parish administrator such as a parish business manager. The controlling function follows up on the organizing function by asking "Who reviews staff performance?" and a related question, "Is staff compensation affected by the performance review process?"

The National Survey of Catholic Parishes asked about performance reviews of paid ministry staff (Table 5.1). Fewer than half of paid ministry staff receive a formal appraisal, and of these, fewer than half had their compensation tied to their appraisal. Those who received an appraisal were most likely to receive it from their pastor. Fifty percent of parishes with a resident pastor say that the paid ministry staff receive a formal performance appraisal. Fifty percent of PLC parishes say the same, but only 33 percent of parishes with a nonresident pastor have a formal performance appraisal for paid ministry staff. Another interesting anomaly: while 44 percent of parishes with a resident pastor tie these performance appraisals to the compensation of their ministry staff, and 39 percent with a nonresident pastor do the same, 63 percent of PLC parishes tie performance appraisal to the compensation of their ministry staff.

A logical next step is for church leaders to implement programs that ensure enough professionally qualified individuals to serve as parish administrators.

THE ROLE OF PARISH BUSINESS MANAGER

Whether or not one accepts the Sweetser model of shared parish leadership, it is clear that the ministry of parish business manager has taken on added importance as Catholic parishes get larger. As mentioned frequently in this book, due to a variety of factors the organizational structure of U.S. Catholic parishes is becoming more complex. It is both unfair and unwise to place a greater administrative burden on pastors, the majority of whom find little personal satisfaction in administration and typically have not received the appropriate education necessary to take on a greater administrative burden (see Conway 1992). The parish model of the future will very likely rely heavily on a professionally trained business manager assisted by a professionally trained and dedicated parish finance council.

The Emerging Models of Parish Leadership Project recognized this fact and included an in-depth study of the role of parish business managers in Phase 2. Data concerning parish business managers were collected from two sources. The Parish Leader Survey conducted by CARA gathered quantitative data from a national sample of parish business managers. These quantitative data were supported by qualitative data collected from four regional focus group sessions. The result was a report, "The Role and Reality of Parish Business Managers and Parish Finance Council Members." Most of the information on parish business managers contained in this section and the material in the following section on parish finance council members is based on this report.

BACKGROUND AND POSITION CHARACTERISTICS

The typical parish business manager (some hold similar titles, such as parish administrator) is a 48-year-old lay woman (62 percent are women). She has a college degree and majored in a business discipline. She has served fewer than 10 years in this position. Her previous professional position was in the financial sector. She had served as a parish volunteer, although one in five had been employed by the parish in another position. She ministers in her home parish. She had been encouraged to apply for the position by either her pastor or a member of the parish staff.

She most likely has a written job description with an annual salary of $43,000, although some earn as much as $98,000, depending on parish size and their responsibilities. She views her role as minimizing the amount of time that the pastor spends on parish temporal issues.

SKILLS: IMPORTANT VERSUS PREPARED

The Emerging Models Study asked a national sample of parish business administrators a series of related questions about skills related to their position in the areas of finances, human resources, general management, legal knowledge, and religious or spiritual preparation. Business managers rated each item on a 4-point scale according to how important each skill is to their position (with 1 indicating "not at all important" and 4 indicating "very important"). They next evaluated each item according to how well prepared they feel (with 1 indicating "not at all prepared" and 4 indicating "very well prepared").

As shown in Table 5.2, of the 26 items listed, in about half (14 items) there was a significant difference in average scores between the importance of an item and the respondents' perceived level of preparation, indicating some serious underpreparation in a number of skill areas.

In many cases it is probable that the respondents underestimated the importance of a particular item, especially as the demands on parish business managers increase moving forward. For example, no one expects business managers to be trained attorneys, but parishes routinely deal in contracts and other civil law issues that require some understanding of legal principles. On a lesser scale this is also true of canon law. As parish staffs grow and the parish business manager takes on more human resources responsibilities, issues such as employment law become more important, but so do standard human resource tasks such as motivating involvement, managing volunteers, performance appraisals, and team building. More complex parish organizational structures will require more sophisticated pastoral planning. As these

Table 5.2 Parish Business Managers' Impression of Skills and Preparation

Average Scores for Importance and Level of Preparation for Each Item			
	Importance	Preparation	Difference
Financial			
Administering a budget*	3.88	3.68	0.20
Financial reporting*	3.90	3.78	0.12
Managing investments	2.51	2.48	0.03
Stewardship/development*	3.41	3.15	0.26
Purchasing	3.48	3.50	−0.02
Human Resources			
Performance appraisals	3.15	2.96	0.19
Team building	3.42	3.28	0.14
Collaboration*	3.65	3.46	0.19
Supervising others	3.55	3.40	0.15
Motivating involvement	3.22	3.05	0.17
Managing volunteers	3.19	3.15	0.04
Conflict resolution*	3.39	2.94	0.45
General Management			
Database management*	3.50	3.27	0.23
Process management	3.08	3.06	0.02
Project management	3.46	3.50	−0.04
Construction management*	2.90	2.57	0.33
Facilities management*	3.59	3.18	0.41
Strategic/pastoral planning*	3.09	2.77	0.32
Church marketing*	2.78	2.50	0.28
Working with boards/councils	3.52	3.56	−0.04
Legal			
Understanding canon law*	2.43	2.09	0.34
Understanding civil law*	2.93	2.69	0.24
Safe environment and security*	3.48	3.22	0.26
Religious			
Possessing a personal spirituality	3.47	3.31	0.16
Catholic social teaching	2.72	2.64	0.08
Understanding Church doctrine*	2.85	2.66	0.19

*Indicates significant difference between mean scores at 95% confidence level.

Source: Conference for Pastoral Planning and Council Development 2014.

responsibilities increase in importance, so does the need for education and training in these areas.

THE ROLE OF PARISH ADVISORY COUNCILS

One obvious difference between the typical parish studied in the Notre Dame Study and the typical parish of today is the role of parish advisory councils, specifically parish finance councils and parish pastoral councils. The Code of Canon Law promulgated in 1983 mentions both types. Parish finance councils are mandated by canon law (canon 537), but it is up to the diocesan bishop as to whether parishes in the diocese are required to have a pastoral council (canon 536.1).

While the two types of advisory councils differ in the extent to which they are required in canon law, there are some similarities. Canons 536.1 and 537 make it clear that these bodies are to be consultative to the pastor. He may or may not accept their advice, and they do not supervise parish staff or ministries. One important difference between the two is the type of knowledge council members should possess. Finance council members should have specific knowledge about financial matters; their decisions should be informed by professional financial standards. Pastoral council members should possess knowledge about the parish and its culture; their decisions should be informed by dialogue with their fellow parishioners.

PARISH FINANCE COUNCILS

Data from the Emerging Models Study reveal that 97 percent of the responding parishes have a finance council. The median number of members is six. Ninety percent of the councils meet at least quarterly, while 7.5 percent meet semiannually or less often.

Finance Council Member Characteristics

The typical parish finance council member is a 61-year-old lay man. He has a college degree (many have graduate or professional degrees). His business experience (nearly all come from a business background) is in the financial sector or in management. He has served for 11 years on the council and was initially recruited by the pastor directly.

What do finance council members do? The Emerging Models Study found that they tended to be involved at one level or another in budgeting, setting parish financial policy, and planning for the parish's long-term financial and physical needs. Table 5.3 shows the frequency with which finance councils in the sample reviewed typical financial statements and their evaluation as to whether that frequency was sufficient for each. With a couple of exceptions, an overwhelming majority of councils reviewed each financial statement at least quarterly, and, with the same exceptions, a majority of the respondents believed their finance councils reviewed these statements with sufficient frequency.

Areas of Responsibility: Important versus Prepared

The Emerging Models Study asked parish finance council members to evaluate (using the same 4-point scale that was used for the parish

Table 5.3 Parish Finance Council Review of Financial Statements

Percentage Responding for Each Item			
	Never	At Least Quarterly	Sufficient
Periodic cash Receipts/disbursements	9	87	60
Balance sheet	1	89	60
Cash on hand	2	90	59
Comparison of actuals to budgeted	3	89	57
YTD cash Receipts/disbursements	6	87	56
Comparison of current to prior year	5	84	56
Debt outstanding	1	85	53
Unpaid bills at end of period	27	64	47
Bank reconciliations	29	62	46
Investment results	9	70	44

Source: Conference for Pastoral Planning and Council Development 2014.

Table 5.4 Parish Finance Council Members' Impression of Skills and Preparation

Average Scores for Importance and Level of Preparation for Each Item			
	Importance	Preparation	Difference
Financial			
Administering a budget*	3.83	3.68	0.20
Financial reporting*	3.82	3.53	0.31
Managing investments	3.01	2.89	0.12
Stewardship/development*	3.37	3.07	0.30
Insurance	2.94	2.78	0.16
Real estate	2.46	2.38	0.08
General Management			
Project management	2.98	3.00	−0.02
Facilities management*	3.24	2.99	0.25
Strategic/pastoral planning*	3.26	2.90	0.36
Church marketing	2.63	2.54	0.09
Legal			
Understanding canon law*	2.44	2.01	0.43
Understanding civil law	2.86	2.64	0.22
Understanding diocesan financial guidelines*	3.65	3.02	0.63

*Indicates significant difference between mean scores at 95% confidence level.

Source: Conference for Pastoral Planning and Council Development 2014.

business managers) the importance of a variety of areas where a pastor might approach the finance council for advice. Just as with the business managers, they were then asked to evaluate how well prepared they feel they are for each area. Table 5.4 displays the results.

Based on the importance they gave to each of seven areas of actual or potential responsibility, the study concluded that respondents feel significantly underprepared. While it is distressing to learn of significant discrepancies between level of importance and degree of preparedness in areas such as budgeting, financial reporting, and strategic planning, it is most disturbing that the respondents indicated that the greatest shortfall in their preparation is in their understanding of diocesan financial guidelines.

Nearly as troubling is the degree to which respondents undervalued the importance of other areas of responsibility, such as insurance and civil law. As parish organizational structures become more complex, finance councils will increasingly be required to have some familiarity with these areas.

PARISH PASTORAL COUNCILS

Parish pastoral councils are not required by canon law; it is up to the diocesan bishop to decide if they will be required in his diocese. In the Emerging Models sample 93 percent of the parishes reported that they have a pastoral council. This varied little by parish organizational structure.

The median number of council members was 12. Consolidated parishes tended to have the largest councils, while multiparish ministries have the smallest.

Parishes used a variety of methods to select council membership. Of those parishes responding, 40 percent selected at least some members through an at-large election; 39 percent selected at least some members through a discernment process; in 49 percent of the parishes at least some members were selected by the pastor or PLC; 26 percent had members sent by parish organizations; and 52 percent had members serving ex officio.

Two-thirds of the pastoral councils met monthly and 96 percent met at least quarterly. PLC parishes and multiparish ministries were least likely to meet monthly but most likely to meet bimonthly or quarterly.

A 2010 study of advisory councils by Zech et al. provides some details on parish pastoral council activities. On the issue of who chairs council meetings, more than 75 percent indicated that meetings were chaired by a council member rather than the pastor or PLC. That was most likely to be the case in PLC parishes, where council meetings were chaired by a council member in over 90 percent of the cases. Irrespective of who chairs the meeting, the pastor and chair collaborated in setting the agenda in more than 50 percent of the parishes, with the pastor setting the agenda by himself in 28 percent of the parishes. Typical agenda items included prayer (84 percent of the parishes), issues for recommendation (80 percent), and committee or ministry reports (75 percent). Fewer than a third of the parishes included formation, faith sharing, social time, or meeting evaluation on the agenda. When asked what the pastoral council's most important function was, the response most frequently listed as "very important" was recommending action to the pastor (65 percent). Other functions identified as very important were setting the parish's vision (63 percent), developing parish community (58 percent), and serving as a sounding board for parish groups (58 percent). Finally, three-fourths of the parishes indicated that they typically employ a group consensus process rather than majority vote to reach their recommendations.

The Emerging Models Study asked parishioners to evaluate their parish council and about their perception of the council members' accessibility to parishioners. Thirteen percent rated their parish's pastoral council as poor or fair, while 43 percent rated it as excellent. When asked about council members' accessibility, 19 percent rated it as poor or fair, while 29 percent rated it as excellent.

CONCLUSION

The Notre Dame Study had little to say about parish administration. Today, though, with larger and more complex parishes (multicultural, nonresident pastor, etc.), administration is a critical component of parish life. The Notre Dame Study was conducted just as the laity began taking on important administrative roles in parishes. As important as those roles may have been in the 1980s, they are critical to parish life today. The growth in the number of Catholics in the United States combined with the decrease in ordained clergy has opened the door for parishioners to assume the parish leadership roles envisioned for them in *Lumen Gentium* and other Vatican II documents. These roles have included serving as PLCs, paid lay staff, members of parish advisory councils, and leaders of other parish ministries. They will likely expand in the future as the parish model of co-responsibility of the laity with the pastor, promulgated by Pope Emeritus Benedict XVI (2009), takes hold in our parishes.

This chapter has focused much of its attention on two roles that have taken on additional significance in recent years: parish business manager and member of a parish advisory council. The Emerging Models Study found that the role of parish business manager has become more professionalized. While some business managers are still hired primarily because they are active parish members, more often newly hired business managers have some prior business experience. That's a good thing, because they are being asked to do more than just bookkeeping. In fact the model of parish administration recommended by Fr. Sweetser envisions the business manager as a partner to the pastor, taking on much of the pastor's governance responsibilities. This includes not only parish finances but also parish facilities and many human resources tasks. At the same time the role of the laity in nonstaff parish ministries has grown. This is notably true in the case of parish advisory councils. While one is required by canon law and the other is not, both parish finance councils and parish pastoral councils are relied upon to provide sound consultative wisdom to pastors. Their roles are distinct (although complementary), and they rely on separate methods for gathering information, but their importance for effective parish administration cannot be overstated.

It is important that the Church, primarily through diocesan structures, invests in the formation and training of both parish business managers and members of parish advisory councils.

CHAPTER SIX

CATHOLIC PARISH FINANCES IN THE 21ST CENTURY

As is the case with parish administration, the Notre Dame Study contained little on the specific topic of parish finances. Yet issues surrounding parish finances have been the driving force in many U.S. Catholic Church decisions, as revenues have been flat and expenses have skyrocketed.

The finances of U.S. Catholic parishes in the latter part of the 20th century and the early 21st have been impacted by three major trends: (1) the relatively low level of giving by Catholic parishioners relative to members of other Christian churches, (2) rising expenditures due to factors such as increased labor costs and facilities maintenance, and (3) the migration of Catholics from urban and farming communities to the suburbs, out of the Northeast and Midwest and into the South and the West (see chapter 2). As a result of these trends the National Survey of Catholic Parishes (2014) found that 24 percent of parishes were operating at a loss in 2013, and 8 percent received a diocesan subsidy for their operations. As disconcerting as this may be, it is an improvement from the comparable figures during and following the great recession that occurred in 2007–9. In 2008, 32.3 percent of U.S. Catholic parishes reported an operating loss, and in 2010 the figure was 29.9 percent, according to the Emerging Models Study. In their attempt to halt the financial bleeding of parishes, many dioceses have resorted to drastic cost-cutting measures, including the closing and merging of parishes and laying off staff.

This chapter examines the revenue and expenditure elements of parish finances nationally, along with other important dimensions of parish finances, such as internal financial controls.

PARISH REVENUE

The largest source of revenue for a typical Catholic parish is the regular weekend offertory collection. This is supplemented by holiday collections, including those held on Easter and Christmas; other collections; and various parish fundraisers. Unfortunately, when it comes to supporting their parish Catholics are notoriously poor givers relative to Protestants.

OFFERTORY COLLECTIONS

Nearly every study of Catholic giving conducted in the late 20th and early 21st centuries has found that Catholics contribute about half as much to their parish, as a percentage of household income, as Protestants contribute to their congregation. The typical Catholic household contributes 1.1 to 1.2 percent of their income, while the typical Protestant household contributes 2.2 to 2.5 percent. In neither group does the average member tithe. But if the typical Catholic household contributed to its parish at just the same rate as the typical Protestant household, the parish would double its revenue, and the lion's share of the financial pressures experienced by most Catholic parishes would vanish. Again this doesn't even require tithing, just the 2.2 to 2.5 percent contributed by Protestants.

The low giving by Catholic parishioners is compounded by the fact that most parishes rely heavily on the collection basket for their contributions, as opposed to other approaches such as tithing or pledging. When Catholics don't attend, they generally don't contribute. The lack of growth in weekend Mass attendance (documented in a previous chapter) along with this overall low giving rate has meant that parish revenues have remained somewhat flat.

There have been a number of empirical studies of giving to Catholic parishes. Most have been centered on the concept of stewardship: the giving of time, talent, and treasure to the parish motivated by a desire to support God's work on earth. Other motives, such as giving out of a sense of commitment to a group (i.e., the parish membership), have also been studied, but the stewardship approach has been the most pervasive.

Several factors have been found to be successful in increasing parishioner contributions. Some are intentionally stewardship-driven, such as including stewardship as part of the parish plan; appointing a stewardship council to lead the parish's stewardship efforts; emphasizing stewardship in parish education programs at all levels; and sponsoring lay witnesses who speak about their stewardship journey. Other successful approaches involve actions that a good parish should be doing anyway and are not intentionally stewardship-driven; these include stressing the importance of being a welcoming place that takes community building seriously, accentuating pledging, and practicing sound financial transparency and accountability (see Zech 2008).

One innovation in church giving has been the use of Electronic Funds Transfer, commonly known as electronic giving. The benefits of EFT include the following:

- Parishioners contribute to the parish usually at the beginning of each month. This is consistent with the "first fruits" concept of stewardship and is the time parishioners can more readily afford a generous contribution.
- Parishioners contribute even if they are absent from Mass because they are ill, on vacation, or for any other reason.
- EFT is a form of pledging and involves making a financial commitment to the parish.

Some pastors oppose the concept of EFT, fearing that it diminishes the importance of the offertory as part of the liturgy. Data from the National Survey of Catholic Parishes reveal that about half of the responding parishes provided their parishioners with the opportunity to contribute online. In the Cooperative Congregational Studies Partnership, another national survey of parishes that was conducted in 2010, 43 percent of responding Catholic parishes indicated that the parish offers EFT or electronic giving as a stewardship option.

DETERMINANTS OF PARISHIONER CONTRIBUTIONS

There are a variety of ways to examine parishioner contributions. Historically researchers have focused on parish characteristics, such as number of members, as well as parishioner characteristics, such as ethnic background and age cohort. More recently researchers have focused on the organizational structure of a parish, especially changes in organizational structure, as a factor in motivating giving.

Contributions Related to Parish Characteristics

Figure 6.1 shows the average weekly giving per household according to the size of the parish. It is not surprising to find that parishioners in small parishes contribute at a significantly higher rate than do parishioners in large parishes. This pattern is typically explained by the "free rider effect." Free riders are those who value what the parish has to offer but contribute little or nothing to support it. Parishioners in small parishes are aware that their individual contributions make up a relatively large portion of the parish budget. They know that if they give only a small amount, or fail to contribute at all, their parish will suffer.

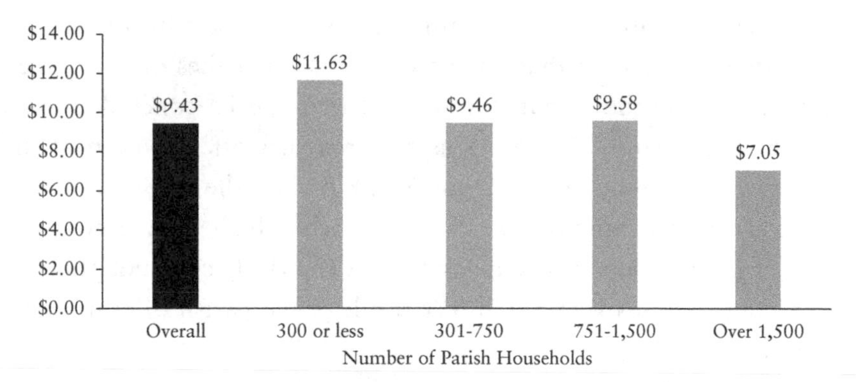

Figure 6.1 Average Weekly Household Giving by Number of Parish Households, 2010

Source: Gray et al. 2011.

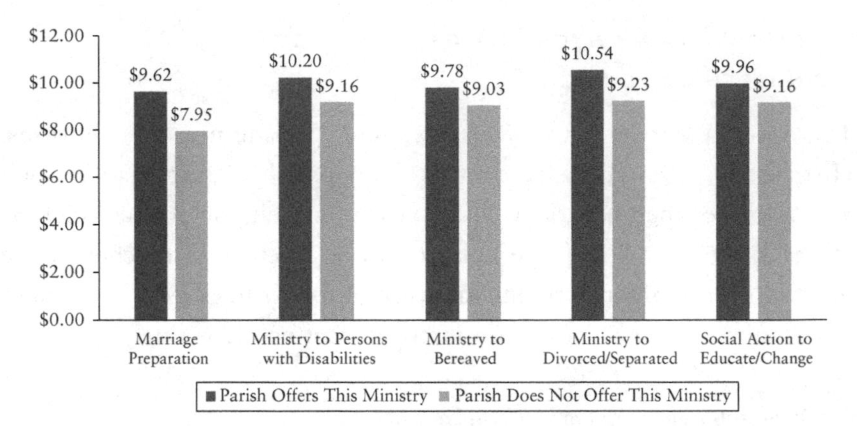

Figure 6.2 Average Weekly Household Giving According to Parish Ministries Offered, 2010.

Source: Gray et al. 2011.

Hence they are less inclined to be free riders. Parishioners in large parishes, however, recognize that their individual contributions make up a relatively small fraction of the parish budget; the parish will barely be affected if they give little or nothing at all, so they take advantage of that situation. A parish can survive with a handful of free riders, but when many parishioners act as free riders the parish suffers financially.

The Emerging Models Study asked about a variety of parish ministries. Those that are shown in Figure 6.2 exhibited statistically significant differences in contributions between those parishes that provided the ministry and those that did not. All that can be concluded from the results, shown in Figure 6.2, is that parishes offering each of the ministries received larger contributions. But since the larger contributions could be the result of other factors (such as higher socioeconomic status of parishioners) it is impossible to definitively conclude that the larger contributions were the direct result of the parish offering these ministries.

Contributions Related to Parishioner Characteristics

Table 6.1 shows the average weekly giving per household broken down by some parishioner characteristics. Differences in giving by ethnic background are all statistically significant except for the case of Asians/ Pacific Islanders. The findings show that parishes with a large percentage of non-Hispanic white parishioners receive significantly higher per household weekly contributions, as do parishes with more than 10 percent African Americans. Parishes with a large percentage of Hispanics receive significantly lower contributions. This latter finding can perhaps be explained by the fact that parishes with large Hispanic populations

Table 6.1 Average per Household Weekly Offertory by Parish Ethnic Composition, 2010

	Per Household
All parishes	$9.43
Ethnic Background	
Multicultural Parish	
Yes	$8.35
No	$10.10
Percent non-Hispanic white	
0 to 80	$7.84
81 to 97.5	$10.07
More than 97.5	$10.32
Percent African American	
0	$9.71
.1 to 10.0	$9.03
More than 10.0	$11.34
Percent Hispanic	
0	$9.82
0.1 to 50.0	$9.84
More than 50.0	$5.59
Percent Asian/Pacific Islander	
0	$9.89
0.1 to 2.0	$9.28
More than 2.0	$8.75

Source: Gray et al. 2011.

often serve many immigrant households from parts of the world where churches are supported by the state, so there is no tradition of individual contributions to the parish. This may also be reflective of the generally lower socioeconomic status of Hispanics in the United States. The larger contributions received by parishes with more than 10 percent African Americans might reflect the influence of historically black churches, where household giving has traditionally outpaced giving in Catholic parishes.

There is a well-developed literature on the impact of age cohorts on religious practices. James Davidson et al. (1997) performed the seminal work showing that religious practices are affected by events that each cohort experienced as it was coming of age. These events shape cohort members' worldview. According to this analysis, each generation not only shares a similar chronological age but also a perception of society and its institutions formed by its members' common experiences. One would expect this would carry over to financial support of the parish. However, examination of these data shows no significant difference in giving by age cohort (not shown in the table).

CONTRIBUTIONS RELATED TO PARISH ORGANIZATIONAL STRUCTURE

Chapter 4 examined parish organizational restructuring, including mergers, priests pastoring multiple parishes, and parishes administered by someone who is not a priest. How do these different organizational structures impact parishioner financial contributions? Figure 6.3 shows the average weekly giving per household broken down by parish organizational structure. Parishioners react to parish organizational changes that might impact the way they experience parish life.

Few parishioners would be excited about their parish being merged, clustered, suppressed, or not assigned a priest to administer it. They express their dissatisfaction in any number of ways, including withholding financial contributions. That would be consistent with the giving data in Figure 6.3 for parishes that had been merged, clustered, or suppressed. However, Figure 6.3 shows that average weekly giving

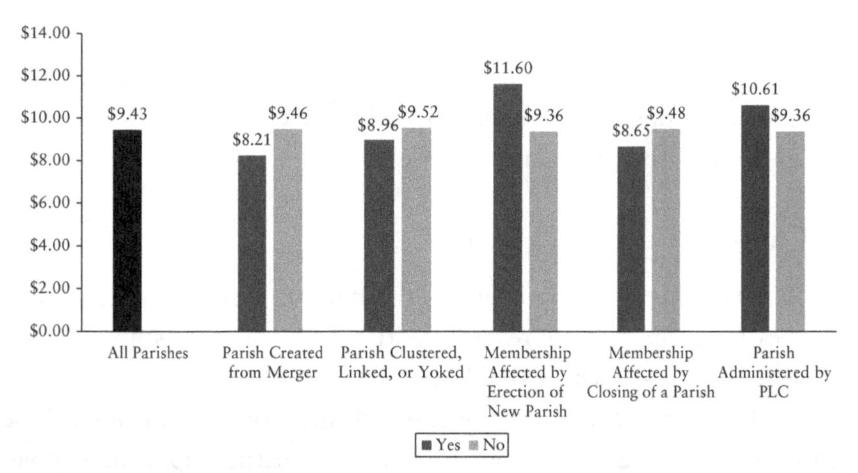

Figure 6.3 Average Weekly Household Giving According to Parish Organizational Structure, 2010.

Source: Gray et al. 2011.

is greater in parishes administered by a parish life coordinator. In the absence of more data one can only speculate on a reason, but it might be that losing a resident priest can bring a parish community closer together. Another explanation could be that bishops are highly selective in choosing PLCs. It is certainly true that parishes led by PLCs tend to be smaller, which enhances the possibilities for community building and reduces free riding. Whatever the reason, organizing a parish as a PLC parish does not carry the same financial liability as other parish organizational structure reconfigurations.

According to Figure 6.3, the same could be said about parishes that were formed by erecting a new parish: they too receive larger contributions. One possible explanation is that parishioners might be excited about the possibilities surrounding something new and thus are more willing to support the new initiative. Or, as alluded to earlier, it could be simply that many new parishes are erected in suburban settings where incomes tend to be higher.

It is important to emphasize that the relationships shown in these tables and figures do not necessarily represent causality; they might simply reflect differences in parishioner socioeconomic status. As chapters 2 and 4 indicated, parish closings, mergers, and clusters are primarily taking place in the urban areas of the Northeast and Midwest, while new parishes are more likely to be formed in the South and West and in the suburbs around major cities.

OTHER REVENUE SOURCES

While the weekly offertory provides the bulk of parish revenues, many parishes supplement their revenue with other collections and a variety of fundraisers, such as building funds and raffles. In 2013 half of all parishes received 8 percent or more of their revenue through these supplementary programs. About 4 percent of parishes report no supplemental revenue. Among the various sorts of parish structures studied in this research, parishes that share a common pastor (e.g., twinned, yoked, clustered) are most reliant on other than offertory collections as a source of revenue. Some 10 percent of these parishes receive half or more of their revenue from sources other than the offertory. Somewhat surprisingly PLC parishes are least dependent on these other sources. None of the PLC parishes reports receiving more than half of its revenue from sources other than the parish offertory. There were no significant differences in nonoffertory revenue according to parish size.

Another source of parish revenue is a subsidy received from the diocese. Diocesan subsidies are typically reserved for parishes that are struggling financially through no fault of their own, such as those located in poorer neighborhoods. The number of parishes requiring a subsidy, and the amount of the subsidy, is also related to the state of the local economy. In 2013, 8 percent of the parishes in the National Survey of Catholic Parishes received a diocesan subsidy with an average amount of $26,892. Of those parishes receiving a subsidy, the average amount was 11 percent of total parish revenue. But the percentage of revenue accounted for by diocesan subsidy differed dramatically by parish size. Among parishes receiving a subsidy, those with fewer than 500 households received an average of 17 percent of their revenue in the form of a subsidy; parishes with more than 500 households received an average of 3.5 percent of their revenue from subsidies. For about a quarter of the parishes receiving subsidies, the amount of the subsidy was 20 percent or more of their total revenue.

PARISH EXPENSES

Based on data from the National Survey of Catholic Parishes, the average parish operating expenses in 2013 were $800,511. Parish expenses have been increasing due to two primary causes. First, many parishes own a considerable number of facilities (church buildings, schools, rectories, etc.) that require regular maintenance. Second, there has been a substantial modification in the parish workforce: where once parishes were staffed almost entirely by clergy, vowed religious, and a few lay volunteers, today they are staffed primarily by paid laity, many with advanced degrees and anticipating compensation in line with their professional status.

FACILITIES

According to the Emerging Models Study, the average parish church building was 61 years old in 2010; nearly a third (31 percent) were more than 80 years old. Church buildings that old are typically accompanied by school buildings and rectories of similar longevity. The maintenance costs on these buildings mount each year. Unfortunately parishes haven't always been timely in maintaining their facilities, so many are faced with significant deferred maintenance outlays.

One of the key factors affecting facilities costs is the mismatch between areas where the facilities are located and the places where much of the Catholic population now resides. At the time when many of these facilities were constructed the Catholic population was heavily concentrated in urban areas, especially in the Northeast and Midwest. Over time that population has migrated to suburban areas and to the South and West. But the facilities still remain in place in urban areas. This has resulted in numerous older, run-down buildings badly in need of maintenance located in areas where Catholics have out-migrated.

They serve a smaller and less affluent Catholic population. This situation has been magnified by the fact that in recent years the United States has experienced a significant immigration of Catholics who have settled primarily in the South and West. All this movement has resulted in the reconfiguration (closure, merger, twinning, etc.) of many urban parishes at the same time funds are sought to construct new facilities in the South and West and in the suburbs of the Northeast and Midwest.

LABOR COSTS

The National Survey of Catholic Parishes data indicate that the average parish employs 4.5 paid staff (full time or part time). Of these, 85 percent are lay men and women, and the remainder are deacons and vowed religious. They tend to be highly educated. The most common degree held by lay ecclesial ministers is a master's in ministry, religion, or theology; 27 percent have this degree in hand, and an additional 8 percent are in progress in a program that will lead to this degree. Twenty-eight percent have a ministry formation program certificate, and 9 percent are in the process of earning this. Twelve percent have a bachelor's degree in ministry, religion, or theology, and an additional 5 percent are in progress in a program that will lead to this degree. Five percent have an associate's degree in ministry, religion, or theology, and 2 percent are working on earning this degree. Only 1 percent has a doctorate in ministry, religion, or theology, and 2 percent are working on earning this degree. Millennial generation lay ecclesial ministers are the most likely to have a bachelor's or master's degree in ministry, religion, or theology (43 percent and 57 percent, respectively).

The median annual pay for lay ecclesial ministers, as reported to CARA by pastors and parish life coordinators in 2010 was $27,590 (Figure 6.4).[1] The minimum annual salary/wages reported was $7,572; the maximum was $89,184.

1. This includes only those lay ministers in pastoral ministries working 20 hours or more per week in paid ministry. The median annual salary/wages reported by lay ecclesial ministers in CARA's 2012 survey of parish leaders for the Emerging Models study was $34,200. However, this may include income from multiple parishes and is based on a smaller sample of individuals than CARA's 2010 survey of parishes for the Emerging Models study.

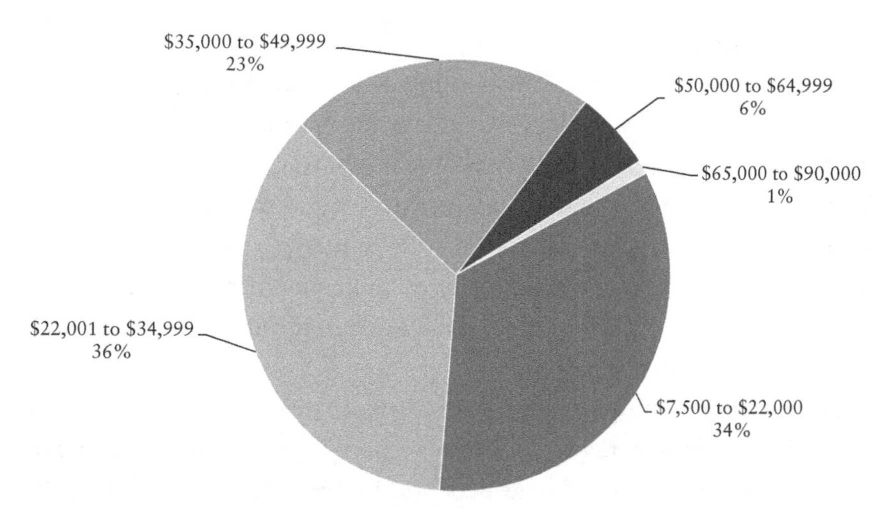

Figure 6.4 Annual Pay for Lay Ecclesial Ministers, 2010.
Source: Gray et al. 2011.

If it were the only income for a family of four, the median annual salary/wages would be $5,477 above the federal poverty line for 2010 (i.e., $22,113). Thirty-four percent of lay ecclesial ministers earn $22,000 or less per year for their ministry.[2] Seventy-one percent of lay ecclesial ministers who are not vowed religious are married.[3] Of those who are married, 89 percent have a Catholic spouse. Eighty-one percent of married lay ecclesial ministers have a spouse who is working. Thus, for many the income they earn is supplemented by a spouse's income.[4]

Nearly all lay ecclesial ministers agree "somewhat" or "very much" that they "feel sufficient job security in the parish" (95 percent and 56 percent agree "very much" only) and that their parish provides them "with the resources I need for my ministry/service" (95 percent and 68 percent agree "very much" only).

2. Twenty-seven percent of lay ecclesial ministers surveyed in 2012 reported ministry and income wages at or below the poverty level for a family of four in that year (Gray et al. 2011).

3. Nineteen percent have never married; 6 percent are separated or divorced; and 4 percent are widowed (Gray et al. 2011).

4. The median household income in lay ecclesial minister households is nearly the same as the median for all U.S. households (Gray et al. 2011).

The average number of hours worked per week by lay ecclesial ministers (i.e., those paid and working at least 20 hours per week), as reported to CARA by pastors and parish life coordinators in 2010, was 34.5. Forty-seven percent of lay ecclesial ministers report that they are involved in ministry in more than one parish and may work additional hours elsewhere (on average about 7.6 hours per week). Sometimes this is in the context of being a shared staff member in a multiparish ministry setting. Twenty-percent of lay ecclesial ministers additionally have paid jobs outside of ministry.

An important component of any employee's compensation comes in the form of fringe benefits. Figure 6.5 shows the percentage of parish staff receiving common fringe benefits. In every case, save for health insurance, the portion of parish staff receiving a specific fringe benefit is greater than that for private-sector employees as a whole. In the case of health insurance the national average is only marginally higher.

Comparing the financial impact of parish staff today with the situation at the time of the Notre Dame Study, there has been an increase in paid parish staff as parishes rely more heavily on trained professionals rather than volunteers to fill lay ecclesial ministry roles. Although they are still underpaid given their level of education, parish workers are far more highly compensated than were the vowed religious who made up a considerable proportion of paid parish staff at the time of the

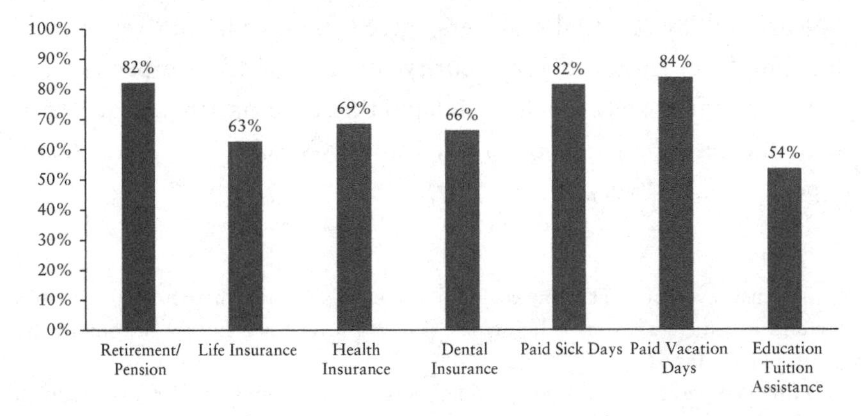

Figure 6.5 Paid Staff Receiving Common Fringe Benefits, 2013.

Source: CARA National Survey of Catholic Parishes 2014.

Table 6.2 Average Percentage of Parish Expenses

Religious education of youth	9%
Faith formation for adults	2%
Worship	5%
School subsidy	
Parochial	25%
Regional	19%

Source: CARA National Survey of Catholic Parishes 2014.

Notre Dame Study. The combination of these factors has significantly impacted parish finances.

OTHER PARISH EXPENSES

The existence of a parish school, either operated solely by the parish or as part of a regional school supported by several parishes in the region, can place a substantial financial burden on a parish. Many parishes find it necessary to subsidize their schools. For context, Table 6.2 shows the average percentage of parish expenditures devoted to some typical parish programs.

For some parishes the subsidy can be financially crippling. According to the CARA National Survey of Catholic Parishes 2014 data, 11 percent of parishes with a parish or regional school spent more than 50 percent of their budget on the school subsidy. Parishes in the Northeast and Midwest, in areas of declining Catholic population, tend to spend a higher proportion of their budget on the school subsidy than do parishes in the South and West.

INTERNAL FINANCIAL CONTROLS

Catholic parishes have always been a tempting target for would-be embezzlers, both clergy and laity. A considerable amount of parish operations are cash-based, and parishes are simply too trusting of parish staff. No one would think that a priest or a lay worker would steal from the Church, so the kinds of internal financial controls that are routine in the business world are often not put into place in parishes. Yet because of the lack of controls some high-profile embezzlements have occurred in recent years, along with many more that didn't make headlines. In fact one study found that over a five-year period 85 percent of U.S. Catholic dioceses had experienced one or more cases of embezzlement (West and Zech 2008).

One of the most effective weapons for discouraging embezzlement is to provide adequate financial transparency to parishioners. They should be kept abreast of parish finances through regular reports issued by the parish finance council. These need not be detailed financial statements, but they should provide enough information so that the interested parishioner can keep track of the parish's financial condition while at the same time shedding enough light on parish finances to dissuade any would-be embezzler.

So, how are parishes doing financially? The Emerging Models Study included two questions for parish leaders related to parish finances: one asked how effective the parish was in managing its finances; the other asked parish leaders whether parishioners were provided with adequate information about parish finances. The findings are shown in Table 6.3.

Generally parish leaders give their parishes high marks for both their ability to manage their finances and for their financial transparency. Parishes that were part of a multiple parish arrangement (yoked, twinned, clustered, etc.) fared slightly better. Parishes headed by a PLC fared worse, although the sample size of leaders from these parishes was relatively small.

Respondents in the Emerging Models Study parishioner survey were also asked if they receive adequate information about finances. A total of 87 percent of parishioners either agreed or agreed strongly with the statement "I feel well-informed about parish finances."

Table 6.3 Parish Leaders' Evaluation of Parish Finances, by Parish Organizational Structure

	"Not at All" or "Only a Little"	"Somewhat" or "Very Much"	"Very Much" Only
All Parishes			
Effective in managing finances	10%	90%	67%
Parishioners have adequate information	13	87	60
Resident Pastor Parishes			
Effective in managing finances	11	90	65
Parishioners have adequate information	14	87	57
Multiple Parish Ministry			
Effective in managing finances	9	91	70
Parishioners have adequate information	10	90	71
Parishes Administered by PLC			
Effective in managing finances	16	84	52
Parishioners have adequate information	25	75	53

Source: Gray 2012.

CONCLUSION

Many U.S. Catholic parishes are in a severe financial situation. Almost a quarter are operating in the red, and many require diocesan subsidies to stay solvent. Low giving by parishioners, coupled with increasing costs and the migration of Catholic populations out of urban and farming communities, have combined to create this condition. In turn this puts financial pressures on dioceses, providing one rationale for dioceses to close or merge parishes, particularly those with aging facilities located in areas with a declining number of Catholics.

And pressure on expenses is not going to subside. Labor costs will only grow as parishes increasingly rely on a well-trained, professional staff requiring appropriate compensation. Facilities costs will increase as church buildings, schools, and rectories age and require increasing maintenance. The long-term financial health of U.S. Catholic parishes depends on their ability to raise more revenue by realizing a higher level of contributions from their parishioners as well as the necessary closing of parishes in areas that no longer have a sufficient population to sustain them. There are a number of avenues that parishes could follow to achieve this goal of increased revenue (guilt? bingo?), but the most promising, and the one most consistent with the mission of the Church, is to emphasize stewardship—the giving of time, talent, and treasure.

However, stewardship is about more than merely contributing treasure, or even time and talent. It is a total way of life, a conversion of mind and heart. It recognizes that all we have is really a gift from God, who asks us to return a portion to support God's work on earth. It is about developing a need to give rather than merely giving to a need.

There are numerous examples of parishes that have turned themselves around financially by becoming "stewardship parishes." All of these have at least two things in common: leadership by a pastor who is truly committed to the concept and the recognition that it will take five years or more for the concept to truly take hold in a parish. Patience to continue the pursuit is essential.

The Emerging Models Study asked parish leaders about stewardship efforts in their parish. Among the respondents, 74 percent agreed "very much" that stewardship should be a priority for their parish, but only 54 percent thought their parish did an excellent job of encouraging stewardship. Much work remains to be done.

CHAPTER SEVEN

WHO'S IN THE PEWS

Just as U.S. society has changed dramatically since the close of the Second Vatican Council in 1965, so too have U.S. Catholics in the pews. Using the Notre Dame Study findings as a comparison point, this chapter examines some of the profound changes among Catholic parishioners that were surveyed for the Emerging Models Study in 2012. As documented in chapter 2, U.S. Catholics are becoming more ethnically and racially diverse, more educated, and more widely dispersed throughout the country than they were at the time of the Notre Dame Study. How does that change play out in parishes?

The primary shifts that have taken place involve changes in ethnic diversity, educational achievement, relationship to the closest parish, weekly Mass attendance, and Catholic school attendance. As we examine these changes over time, we also explore the demographic and religious characteristics of U.S. Catholics in the pews and compare them to all U.S. Catholics nationally, using survey data that CARA has compiled from its national Catholic polls. To illustrate these changes concretely, we summarize the differences by describing the attributes of a "typical" person at a weekend Mass in the United States in 2012 and compare this person to the "typical" parishioner surveyed in the Notre Dame Study.

PARISHIONER DEMOGRAPHICS

We make some comparisons here between the parishioners described as "core Catholics" in the Notre Dame Study (Gremillion and Castelli 1987: 30ff) and the parishioners surveyed in 2012 for the Emerging

Models Study. The two populations are not identical, but the methodology is similar enough for some basic comparisons.[1]

AGE AND GENERATION

In terms of age, the parishioners in the Notre Dame Study averaged just under 50. Parishioners in the Emerging Models Study were about the same age, with an average of 53.

About 50 percent of the Catholic parishioners surveyed in the pews for the Emerging Models Study are of the post–Vatican II and millennial generation; 10 percent are millennial Catholics, born after 1982. The median age of the Catholics surveyed in the pews is 52, which means that half of the Catholics surveyed are under and half are over 52. Keeping in mind that these younger generations of Catholics are also much more racially and ethnically diverse than the generations before them (see Figure 2.4), when we break out the age distribution of parishioners according to their race or ethnic identity (in Figure 7.1), we see even more clearly the increasing diversity in the Catholic population.

ETHNICITY, GENERATION, AND LANGUAGE

It is not possible to compare race and ethnicity of parishioners between the two studies because the Notre Dame Study excluded Spanish-speaking congregations (Gremillion and Castelli 1987: 53ff) and oversampled black Catholics (32). The Emerging Models Study was deliberate in offering the parishioner survey in multiple languages, and 9 percent of those responding chose to take the survey in Spanish. In this study 67 percent of parishioners identified as white, 17 percent

1. Phase 2 of the Notre Dame Study involved a survey sent to 4,555 "scientifically selected parishioners" at 36 parishes, chosen as representative of the 1,099 parishes that responded to the Phase 1 survey. See the appendix for a description of the methodology used for selecting the parishioners surveyed in the Emerging Models Study.

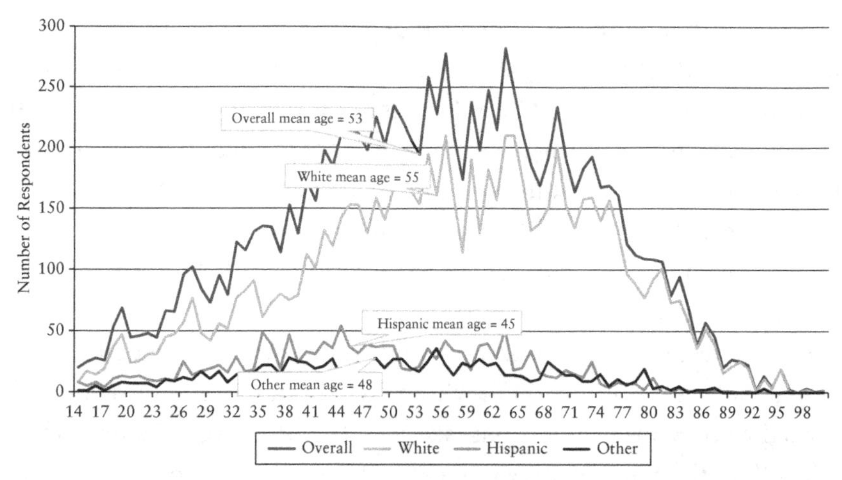

Figure 7.1 Age Distribution of In-Pew Respondents by Race, 2012.
Source: Gray et al. 2013.

as Hispanic/Latino, 11 percent as Asian/Pacific Islander, 3 percent as black/African American, and 3 percent as Native American or other.

That one of the most profound changes among those in the pews over the past twenty-five years is a change that we cannot document just reinforces how dramatic that change has been. The Notre Dame Study, which surveyed registered parishioners in 36 parishes across the country, excluded Hispanic-dominated parishes from participation. The researchers' rationale—that such ethnic groups merited a separate study—would not be accepted in today's Church and would seriously undermine their findings being viewed as representative of the U.S. Catholic Church.

As the 2012 Emerging Models Study in-pew survey of parishioners demonstrates, non-Hispanic whites (67 percent) still make up the majority of those in the pews on a weekend, but Hispanics/Latino(a)s (17 percent) and Asians or Pacific Islanders (11 percent) now also constitute sizable minorities. And although smaller in proportion, non-Hispanic blacks, American Indians, and Alaska Natives should not be neglected either.

Examining the ethnic makeup of the different generations in the pew demonstrates these trends. White respondents, 66 percent of CARA's in-pew Catholics, are most likely among the ethnic groups to be of the pre–Vatican II generation, the oldest of the generations. In contrast 68 percent of Hispanics/Latino(a)s and 61 percent of Asians/Pacific Islanders are found in the two younger generations. Black Catholics, on the other hand, are almost evenly divided between the two younger (54 percent) and two older (46 percent) generations.[2] This increased ethnic diversity among the younger generations is likely to have a long-lasting impact on parish life into the future.

A key question not answered by these data is to what extent the millennials, a larger proportion of whom have been identifying as nonreligious than previous generations (see, e.g., Pew Research Center 2015a), will follow the path of previous generations and become more active in their parishes as they age, get married, and have children. It remains to be seen whether this difference among millennials is truly a generational change or is due to their stage in the life cycle.

The gaps between the ethnic groups present among U.S. Catholics nationally (as described in chapter 2) and those in the pews add another wrinkle to the story of increasing ethnic diversity in the Church. Hispanics/Latino(a)s are estimated to compose 33 percent of all U.S. Catholics but represent only 17 percent of all in-pew respondents. In comparison, non-Hispanic whites make up 60 percent of Catholics nationally but 67 percent of those in pew. The reason Hispanics/Latino(a)s are underrepresented in the pews relative to their proportion of the overall U.S. Catholic population merits further study.

These in-pew Catholics also differ in the languages they use at home: 87 percent say the primary language used at home is English;[3] for 9 percent it is Spanish. Four percent identify an "other" language, the most common being Tagalog.

2. Compared to Catholics nationally, in-pew Catholics are overrepresented among those of the oldest generation (18 percent in pew compared to 10 percent nationally) and underrepresented among millennials (8 percent in pew compared to 23 percent nationally).

3. The Notre Dame Study did not ask about the language(s) spoken in the home.

Examining these findings by ethnic group, 57 percent of Hispanics/Latino(a)s in pew identify Spanish as the primary language used in their homes, with an additional 42 percent identifying English. Among Asian/Pacific Islander respondents, 55 percent identify English, 32 percent Tagalog, and 5 percent Vietnamese.

In general, the older the generation, the more likely its members are to report English as the primary language in their home. Having English as the primary language is highest among the oldest generation (94 percent), declining to 76 percent among the youngest generation. Correspondingly about 15 percent of those of the younger two generations report Spanish as their household's primary language, compared to 3 to 8 percent of those of the oldest two generations.

GENDER AND MARITAL STATUS

The gender of respondents in pew is one area where there has *not* been much change. While the male-to-female ratio currently is about even for Catholics nationally (51 percent female), women make up 64 percent of those in the pews. This is only slightly higher than the 61 percent female population among Mass-attending parishioners estimated in the Notre Dame Study (Leege and Trozzolo 1987: 5).

In-pew Catholics are more likely than Catholics nationally to be married (70 percent compared to 62 percent) and less likely to never have married (15 percent compared to 24 percent). Similar percentages of these two groups report being divorced or separated (8 to 9 percent) or widowed (5 to 7 percent). The higher percentage of married Catholics in pew supports the dominant narrative that Catholics fall away from attending Sunday Mass and being active parishioners as young adults but gravitate back after they marry and have children (see, e.g., Pew Research Center 2015b).

Marital status among Catholic parishioners has changed only a little between the mid-1980s and 2012. Some 73 percent of core Catholics in the Notre Dame Study were married or remarried (compared to 70 percent of Emerging Models Study in-pew Catholics), and 10 percent were never married (compared to 15 percent among in-pew Catholics in 2012). Catholics in these two studies are similar in the percentage divorced or separated (6 percent compared to 8 percent) and widowed (11 percent compared to 5 percent; Gremillion and Castelli 1987: 33).[4]

Currently the greatest differences in marital status exist among those of the various generations. Millennial in-pew Catholics (76 percent) are particularly likely to have never married; those of the post–Vatican II (81 percent) and Vatican II (79 percent) generations are most likely to be married; and those of the pre–Vatican II generation (28 percent) are most likely to be widowed.

Differences in marital status by ethnicity are significant but less dramatic among these in-pew Catholics. As was noted earlier, Hispanic/Latino(a) Catholics in pew are especially likely to belong to the youngest generation of Catholics. Consistent with that finding, Hispanics/Latino(a)s are most likely to have never married (22 percent) and least likely to be married (63 percent). At the other end of the spectrum, non-Hispanic whites are most likely to be married (73 percent) and least likely to never have married (12 percent).

We do not have corresponding data for Catholics nationally or across time, but 39 percent of those responding in pew in 2012 report having at least one child or stepchild under age 18 living with them. Almost half (47 percent) of 2012 in-pew Catholics ages 25 to 34 say they have at least one child or stepchild living with them; 79 percent of those 45 to 54 and 63 percent of those ages 45 to 54 say the same.

LEVEL OF EDUCATION

Compared to core Catholics from the Notre Dame Study, parishes in 2012 have greater success engaging the college educated. As can be seen in Figure 7.2, parishioners from the Notre Dame Study are about half as likely as those in pew in 2012 to have a bachelor's or graduate degree and are about twice as likely to have a high school diploma or less (Gremillion and Castelli 1987: 34). This represents a major shift and is occurring despite Hispanics/Latino(a)s having an overall lower level of education.

4. Note that Gremillion and Castelli do not report the number of core Catholics who were widowed; that figure was imputed from the reported data.

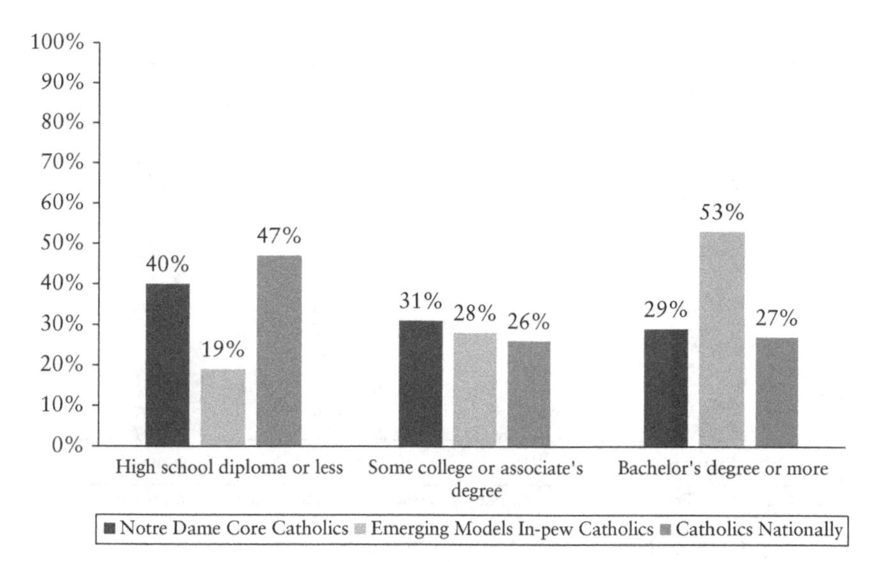

Figure 7.2 Catholics' Highest Level of Education Attained, 1985 and 2012.

Source: Gremillion and Castelli 1987 (Notre Dame Core Catholics), Gray et al. 2013 (Emerging Models In-pew Catholics), CARA 2012 (Catholics Nationally).

Examining just the 2012 findings from Figure 7.2, in-pew Catholics are about twice as likely as all Catholics nationally to have earned at least a bachelor's degree. On the other hand, Catholics nationally are more than twice as likely as Catholics in pew to have attained a high school diploma or less.

Figure 7.3 compares the same education levels for in-pew Catholics by ethnicity. This figure shows Hispanic parishioners having the least education; a plurality has a high school diploma or less (42 percent). Non-Hispanic blacks (71 percent) and Asians (66 percent) are most likely to have a bachelor's or graduate degree, as do most non-Hispanic white parishioners (56 percent).

Educational achievement also varies by generation. Excepting the millennial generation, which has the greatest number of members who have not yet finished their education due to their age, the trend is toward higher educational attainment for each subsequent generation. While 34 percent of the pre–Vatican II generation have a bachelor's or graduate degree, 53 and 63 percent of the Vatican II and post–Vatican II generations have the same, respectively.

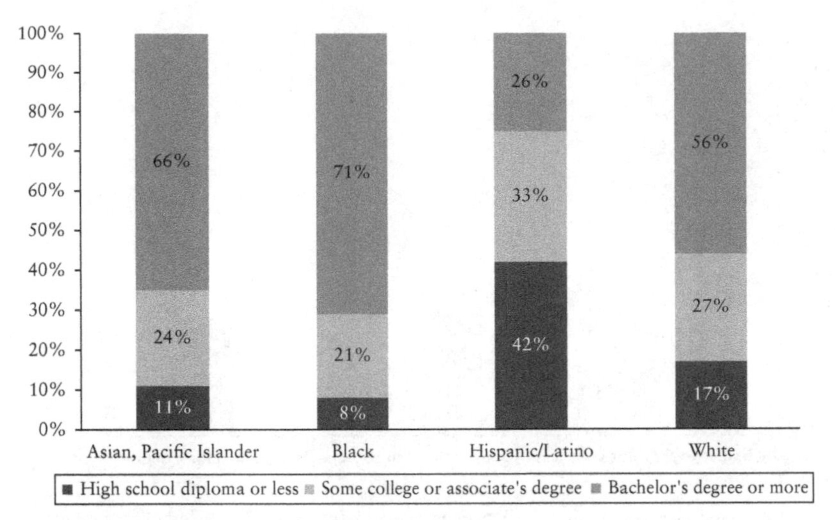

Figure 7.3 Level of Education of In-pew Catholics, 2012, by Ethnicity.

Source: Gray et al. 2013.

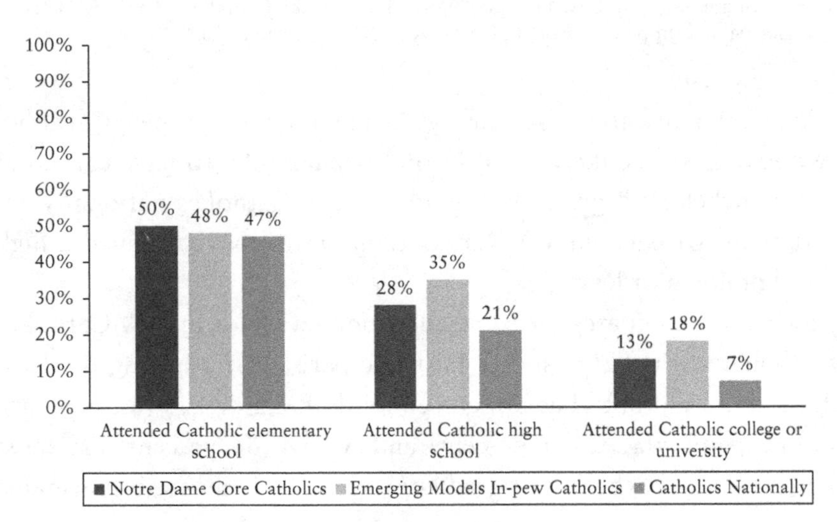

Figure 7.4 Catholic School Attendance, by Survey.

Sources: Gremillion and Castelli 1987 (Notre Dame Core Catholics), Gray et al. 2013 (Emerging Models In-pew Catholics), CARA 2012 (Catholics Nationally).

CATHOLIC EDUCATION

Compared to core Catholics from the Notre Dame Study, 2012 Catholics in pew are about equally likely to have attended a Catholic elementary school but are more likely to have attended a Catholic high school or college. As can be seen in Figure 7.4, a similar pattern holds

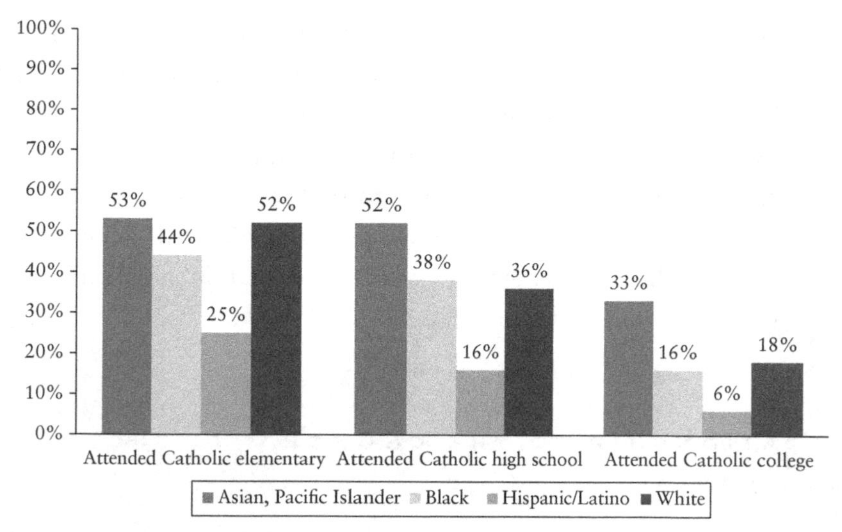

Figure 7.5 In-pew Catholics' Catholic School Attendance, 2012, by Ethnicity.
Source: Gray et al. 2013.

in 2012 for in-pew Catholics and for all Catholics nationally. Thus, while the relationship cannot be said to be causal based on the data presented here, the evidence does support the argument that attending Catholic high schools and colleges impacts whether one will be in the pews later in life (Perl and Gray 2007). This evidence holds for both the Notre Dame Study and the Emerging Models Study.

Subgroup differences are most pronounced among the various ethnic groups. As is shown in Figure 7.5, Asians or Pacific Islanders are most likely to have attended Catholic school at any of the three levels, and Hispanics/Latino(a)s are least likely to have done so.

Catholic school attendance among in-pew Catholics also varies significantly by generation. Sixty percent of Catholics in pew of the oldest generation have ever attended a Catholic school at some point in their lives, compared to 42 percent of those of the youngest generation. There are other differences:

- More than 50 percent of those in the oldest two generations have attended a Catholic elementary school, compared to 41 percent of those in the post–Vatican II generation and 35 percent of millennials.

- Forty percent of the two oldest generations have attended a Catholic high school, compared to 30 percent of the post–Vatican II generation and 26 percent of millennials.
- Twenty percent of those in the two oldest generations have attended a Catholic college, compared to 17 percent of the post–Vatican II generation and 11 percent of millennials. This difference is a little misleading, though, as many millennials may not yet have completed their education.

RELATIONSHIP TO THE CHURCH AND PARISH

Seventy-four percent of Catholics in pew in 2012 identify themselves as active Catholics since birth; 11 percent each identify as a returned Catholic or a convert to Catholicism; and 2 percent each identify as an inactive Catholic or as a non-Catholic.

Some 79 percent of in-pew Catholics in 2012 report being registered at the parish where they responded to the survey. Unfortunately, whether they are registered somewhere else was not asked. In comparison 56 percent of Catholics nationally report being registered at a Catholic parish, whether or not that is the parish they most regularly attend.

As is seen in Figure 7.6, those of different ethnicities tend to have different relationships to the parish where they responded to the 2012 survey. Whites are most likely to have responded at a parish at which they are registered, and Hispanics/Latino(a)s and Asians or Pacific Islanders are least likely.

These data reflect a phenomenon known as "parish hopping" or "parish shopping" that is becoming increasingly common in larger urban and suburban areas where Catholic parishes are located in close proximity. Rather than attending the parish in which they reside, Catholics may choose to attend another parish nearby that better meets their needs or preferences. Perhaps the parish closest to home does not

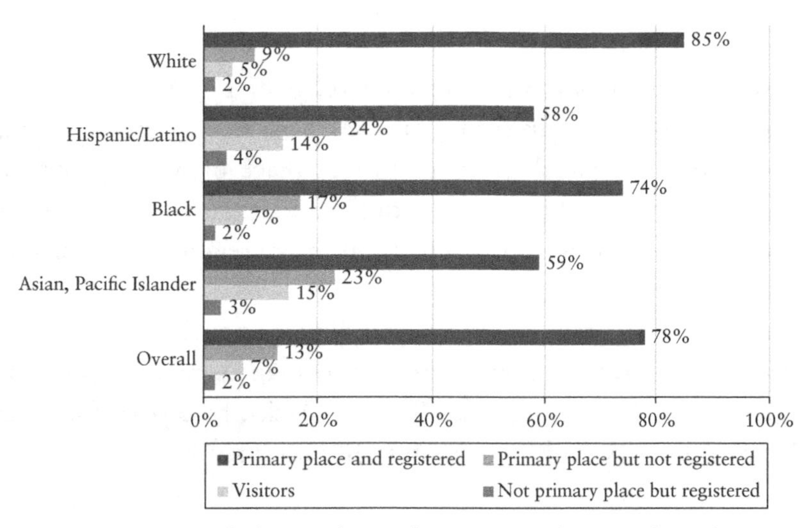

Figure 7.6 In-pew Catholics' Relationship to a Parish, 2012, by Ethnicity.
Source: Gray et al. 2013.

offer an evening Mass, or does not have the style of music you prefer, or has a celebrant who speaks with an accent that is difficult to understand. Instead of putting up with or grumbling about the status quo, Catholics today regularly drive past the parish closest to their home to attend the parish they prefer.

The Emerging Models Study found that nonwhite respondents are most likely to engage in parish hopping. While 29 percent of white parishioners report that they currently live closer to another parish, fully 48 and 47 percent of Hispanics/Latino(a)s and Asians or Pacific Islanders, respectively, report the same. And, although it cannot be tested in the data here, some of those nonwhite respondents doubtless travel to parishes whose parishioners and staff members share their culture and language.

Finally, parish registration also varies by generation: 63 percent of millennials in pew are registered at the parish where they responded to the survey, compared to 85 percent or more of other generations. Some of this drop can be explained by life cycle (i.e., young adults still in school or just starting careers and not attending Mass regularly until they are married with children), but some may be due to other factors as well.

YEARS ATTENDING THE PARISH

In-pew Catholics report attending an average of 13.7 years at the parish where they were surveyed.[5] Among these same Catholics, those reporting that the parish is their primary place of worship but that they are not registered there have attended that parish for an average of 6.4 years. This suggests that such an informal relationship with one's parish can continue for many years.

Some ethnic differences in years attending the parish also exist. Non-Hispanic whites report attending their parish an average of 15.8 years, compared to 13.0 years for non-Hispanic blacks, 10.0 years for Asians or Pacific Islanders, and 8.5 years for Hispanics/Latino(a)s.

MASS ATTENDANCE

National-level data provide evidence of some decrease in frequency of Mass attendance in the more than 50 years since the Second Vatican Council, although a doubling in the overall number of U.S. Catholics during that same period would still suggest a relatively high demand for sacraments. Polling data from 1965 (CARA Frequently Requested Church Statistics) reported that 55 percent of Catholics nationally said they had attended Mass in the previous week, compared to 41 percent in 1985 (the approximate time of the Notre Dame Study) and 24 percent in 2010 (close to the time of the Emerging Models Study in-pew survey of parishioners).

Both the Notre Dame Study and the Emerging Models Study surveyed parishioners, who are more likely than Catholics in general to be regular Mass attenders. Among the core Catholics of the Notre Dame Study, some 72 percent reported attending Mass weekly, compared to 68 percent of those surveyed in pew by the Emerging Models Study. Figure 7.7 compares weekly Mass attendance among the core Catholics of the Notre Dame Study to the Catholics surveyed in pew for the Emerging Models Study by age groups (the only way the Notre

5. The Notre Dame Study did not report the average number of years their core Catholics had attended their parish.

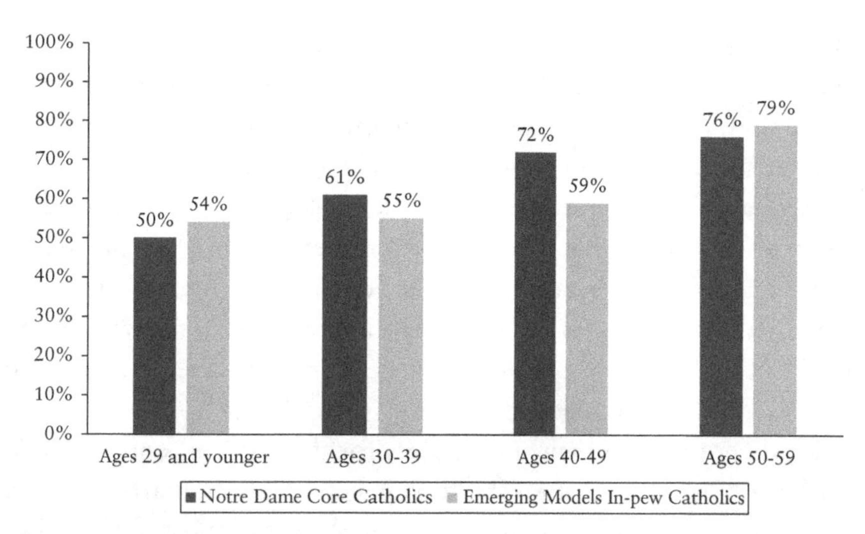

Figure 7.7 Catholics Reporting Weekly Mass Attendance, by Age Group.

Sources: Gremillion and Castelli 1987 (Notre Dame Core Catholics), Gray et al. 2013 (Emerging Models In-pew Catholics).

Dame study presented its data). The only age group that is significantly less likely to report weekly Mass attendance is those in their 40s.

As was likely also the case in 1987, the greatest differences in 2012 appear between Catholics nationally and in-pew respondents. According to CARA polls, 24 percent of Catholics nationally attend Mass weekly or more, compared to 68 percent of Catholics in pew. Moreover, whereas 51 percent of Catholics nationally attend Mass a few times a year or less, only 2 percent of in-pew Catholics report attending that infrequently.

The Emerging Models Study also asked parishioners about Confirmation, although the question was not asked of core Catholics in the Notre Dame Study. Ninety-two percent of in-pew Catholics report having been confirmed. More than 90 percent of those in the oldest three generations have received the sacrament, compared to 81 percent of millennials.

CONCLUSION

One concise way to summarize the findings from this chapter is to describe the attributes of the "typical" Mass attender from the Emerging

Models Study and compare that person to the "typical" core Catholic of the Notre Dame Study. To do so we have to choose the most common characteristic rather than one that characterizes a majority of parishioners. As such, the typical person in the pew in 2012 is a married female with a bachelor's degree between the ages of 45 to 54—a member of the post–Vatican II generation. She identifies as non-Hispanic white, and English is the primary language spoken in her home. She is registered at her primary place of worship and attends Mass every week. She has been an active Catholic since her birth and attended Catholic schools at least for a time.

We do not have as many data points for the "typical" core Catholic from the Notre Dame Study, but this person is also a married female who attended Catholic schools at least for a while, is registered at her parish, and attends Mass weekly. She differs from the typical 2012 in-pew Catholic in that she is slightly younger and has not attended college. In short, she is more similar to than different from the 2012 in-pew respondent.

Ethnic differences matter greatly among the 2012 Catholics, most prominently in terms of Catholic school attendance, relationship to their closest parish, generation, and educational level. As the United States in general and the U.S. Catholic Church in particular continue to become more ethnically diverse, those differences will continue to affect parish life in ways that we can only imagine at this time.

Generational differences will also affect parish life into the future. Millennials, for example, at this time appear to have a somewhat weaker attachment to their parish than do older generations and are also less likely to attend Mass weekly. Whether their rates of parish attachment and Mass attendance increase as they age, as has been the case for previous generations, remains to be seen.

The next chapter explores the increasing diversity in parish life and the way this diversity is being lived out in ethnic parishes and in increasingly multicultural parishes. This increasing diversity is the future of Catholic parish life.

CHAPTER EIGHT

CULTURAL DIVERSITY IN PARISH LIFE

The primary source for the Notre Dame Study's chapter "The Hispanic Community and the Parish" was data from the National Pastoral Center for Hispanics (Gremillion and Castelli 1987: 98). As the authors noted, "Given the distinctive character of Hispanics as a religio-cultural community, their history, and continuing influx from Latin America, the Notre Dame study chose to exclude Spanish-speaking congregations" (77–78). The researchers cite the complications of Spanish translations, Spanish-speaking on-site visitors, and lack of scholars with expertise in "Hispanic culture and religiosity" (78). At the time the researchers estimated that about 2,800 parishes in the United States had "significant numbers of Hispanics" and about 2,500 had Spanish-language Masses (78).

The Notre Dame researchers discussed cultural diversity in the Church primarily as a social context involving Hispanic and non-Hispanic white parishioners. In the 1980s the foreign-born Catholic population numbered between four and five million and accounted for just over 10 percent of Catholics. Waves of immigration that followed increased this population to 16.8 million in 2014, and now more than 25 percent Catholics are born outside the United States (Figure 8.1).

Although much of this immigration is from Latin America, primarily Mexico, other Catholic immigrants have come from dozens of countries across Asia and Africa. The cultural diversity that this has created in the Church cannot be ignored in the 21st century. Rather in many ways it represents the future of the Church in the United States, and the culturally diverse parish is a window into that emerging social context.

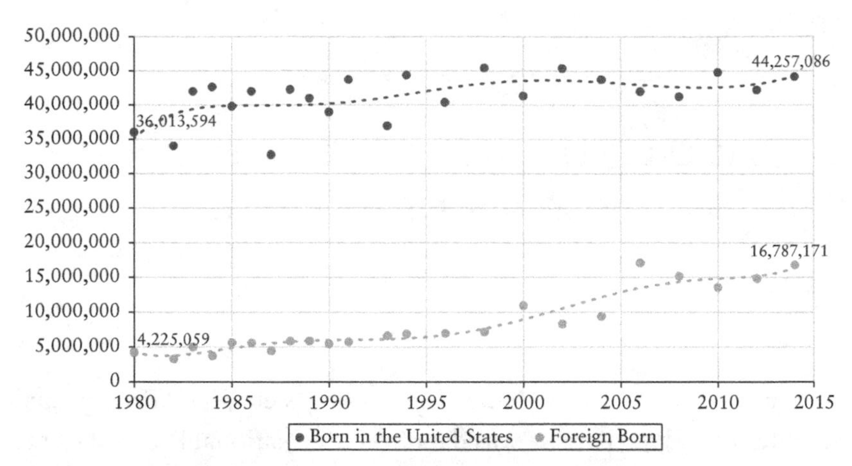

Figure 8.1 U.S.- and Foreign-Born Catholics in the United States, 1980–2014.
Source: Smith et al. 2015, General Social Survey, relevant years; U.S. Census Bureau, International Data Base, relevant years.

Excluding Spanish-speaking congregations from a book on Catholic parish life, let alone those speaking Vietnamese, Tagalog, Korean, Ilocano, Igbo, French, or Chinese, would be an unacceptable choice now. As the 21st century passes the middle of its second decade, the Catholic Church in the United States is one of the most racially, ethnically, culturally, and linguistically diverse religious communities that has ever existed here. In 2013 CARA researchers estimated the size and distribution of black or African American, Asian American or Pacific Islander, Hispanic or Latino(a), and American Indian or Alaskan Native Catholic populations in the United States, as well as the locations of Catholic parishes known to serve these communities (Gray 2015b).

CARA located parishes that self-identify as serving or are known to serve racial, ethnic, cultural, and/or linguistic groups in the United States by combining a dozen databases of parish addresses and information, including some provided by the Secretariat for Cultural Diversity in the Church from the U.S. Conference of Catholic Bishops. CARA then cleaned the database of duplicates and updated any missing or incorrect information to come up with a final database of 6,332 parishes that are known to serve a particular racial, ethnic, cultural, and/or linguistic community

(35.9 percent of all U.S. parishes).[1] Some of these parishes serve two or even more of these communities. Accounting for this additional complexity within parishes, a total of 6,570 communities were identified.

In August 2014 CARA began conducting in-pew surveys with parishioners at randomly selected parishes (Gray 2015b) that had been identified by CARA as among the 6,332 parishes known to be serving diverse communities.[2] CARA translated the survey into 20 different languages that were requested by the pastors in selected parishes. The preliminary results of this endeavor reported here are from the respondents in 27 parish communities that responded as of October 2015. A total of 11,044 teens and adults completed a survey in these 27 parish communities. The sample includes four parishes serving primarily Hispanic or Latino(a) communities; four serving primarily black, African American, African, or Afro-Caribbean communities; six serving primarily Asian, Native Hawaiian, or other Pacific Islander communities; seven serving American Indian or Native Alaskan communities; and six multicultural parishes serving multiple racial, ethnic, cultural, or linguistic communities.

The current sample includes 2,570 respondents who self-identify as Hispanic or Latino(a) as well as 3,625 who self-identify as Asian, Native Hawaiian, or other Pacific Islander.[3] A total of 1,153 self-identify as black, African American, African, or Afro-Caribbean and 365 identify as American Indian or Native Alaskan. A total of 2,142 are non-Hispanic white. Finally, 1,189 identify their race or ethnicity as something else or did not respond to this question.

1. Among the European and "other" parishes are parishes that serve French Canadians as well as parishes that serve specific communities within nations, such as Bohemians and Alsatians.

2. Stratification is used in the sampling to ensure geographic representation as well as reaching the broadest number of racial, ethnic, cultural, and linguistic groups.

3. Respondents provided their race or ethnicity, place of birth, and language used at home. Using all of these pieces of information, CARA identified subgroups of respondents. Multiracial respondents selected more than one race group (excluding Hispanic or Latino(a), an ethnicity).

Table 8.1 Primary Language used at Home

	Frequency	Percentage
English	5,046	46%
Spanish	1,788	16
Tagalog	1,201	11
Vietnamese	270	2
Ilocano	238	2
Korean	142	1
Igbo	109	1
Creole	87	1
French	59	0.5
Chinese, Cantonese, Mandarin	44	0.4
Indonesian	41	0.4
Choctaw	38	0.3
Japanese	28	0.3
Visayan	28	0.3
Polish	22	0.2
Navajo	17	0.2
Yupik	17	0.2
Cebuano	13	0.1
Portuguese	11	0.1
Other languages or unknown	1,845	17

Source: Gray 2015b

Overall 51 percent of respondents in these parishes indicate they were been born outside the United States. All respondents, regardless of place of birth, were asked, "What is the primary language used in your home?" Seven options were provided, along with an "other" option so the respondent could specify a language that was not listed. A majority of respondents did *not* indicate use of English as the primary language at home. Table 8.1 lists the 19 most frequently mentioned languages used by respondents at home (i.e., those specified by at least 10 respondents).[4]

4. Note that about 1,700 respondents did not answer this language question.

COMMUNITY AND DIVERSITY IN THE PARISH

The survey asked parishioners about their agreement with statements regarding community and diversity in their parish. Table 8.2 presents the percentage of respondents who "strongly" agree with each of these statements, according to their self-identified race and ethnicity. Majorities of all subgroups "strongly" agree that having people of different cultural backgrounds enriches their parish: 70 percent or more who self-identify as Hispanic, Asian, or black; 64 percent of non-Hispanic white parishioners; and 58 percent of American Indian parishioners. Most also "strongly" agree that their parish is multicultural, though non-Hispanic white parishioners are more likely to do so than any other subgroup.

Because the statements "Parishioners worship and share together as one community" and "Parishioners of different cultures participate in parish life together" are closely related one would expect the same rate of agreement with both. However, this was not the case (Table 8.2). The second statement, which specifies "parishioners of different cultures," received lower levels of strong agreement among all subgroups. Majorities of all groups except non-Hispanic white parishioners "strongly" agree that parishioners worship and share together as one community. About 50 percent of Hispanic, Asian, and black parishioners "strongly" agree that parishioners of different cultures participate in parish life together, but only 36 percent of American Indian and 37 percent of non-Hispanic white parishioners respond so.

At least half of respondents from each ethnic group except American Indians and Native Alaskans "strongly" agree that they would like to see more diversity in their parish. Only 37 percent of American Indian and Native Alaskans respondents answer this way.

Two other questions gauge how comfortable parishioners feel in their parish community. The first asks if they feel like an outsider because of their nationality, race, ethnicity, language, or culture. The second is broader and asks if there is tension between different cultural groups in the parish. Generally few parishioners "strongly" agreed with

Table 8.2 Community and Parish Diversity

Percentage Responding "Strongly Agree"					
How Much do You Agree with the Following Statements?	Hispanic	Asian	Black	American Indian	Non-Hispanic white
Having people of different cultural backgrounds enriches this parish	77	71	77	58	64%
The parish is multicultural	65	65	63	50	74
Parishioners worship and share together as one community	57	60	63	52	47
I would like to see more diversity in the parish	50	55	56	37	52
Parishioners of different cultures participate in parish life together	48	50	50	36	37
I often feel like an outsider at this parish because of my nationality, race, ethnicity, language, or culture	18	10	9	13	8
There is some tension between different cultural groups in the parish	17	10	10	13	9

Due to limited space in the tables, the names of subgroups have been abbreviated. For example, the column labeled "Black" includes those who self-identify as black, African American, African, and Afro-Caribbean. The "Asian" column includes those who self-identify as Asian, Native Hawaiian, or as Pacific Islander. American Indian includes Native Alaskans.

Source: Gray 2015b

these statements. In part this may reflect the self-selected nature of parish communities. Those who did strongly agree with either statement would likely seek out another parish where they did not feel as uncomfortable. However, among those who are foreign-born and Hispanic, 22 percent "strongly" agree that they often feel like an outsider in their parish, and 20 percent agree that there is some tension between different cultural groups in their parish.

PARISH PRIORITIES

Respondents were also asked to evaluate different priorities for their parish that might relate to cultural diversity. As shown in Table 8.3, most parishioners who are Hispanic, Asian, or black "strongly" agree that their parish should be more involved in providing support for the poor and marginalized, providing assistance to immigrants, providing pastoral care to migrants, improving the sense of community among

Table 8.3 Parish Cultural Diversity Priorities

Percentage Responding "Strongly Agree"					
My Parish Should Be More Involved in ...	Hispanic	Asian	Black	American Indian	Non-Hispanic white
Providing support for the poor and marginalized	74	64	70	59	43%
Providing assistance to immigrants	68	52	55	25	21
Providing pastoral care for refugees	65	49	52	28	22
Improving the sense of community among parishioners	65	64	61	52	43
Celebrating cultural diversity	55	52	55	39	21
Understanding the different cultures that exist within the parish community	54	53	49	39	21

Source: Gray 2015b

parishioners, celebrating cultural diversity, and understanding the different cultures that exist within the parish community.

In contrast, fewer than half of non-Hispanic white parishioners in these diverse parishes agree with other parishioners on these matters. Only slightly more than one in five "strongly" agree that more assistance should be provided to immigrants and refugees and that more should be done to celebrate cultural diversity or to understand different

Table 8.4 Parishioner Attitudes about Welcoming

Percentage Responding "Strongly Agree"					
My Parish Should Be More Involved in Welcoming . . .	Hispanic	Asian	Black	American Indian	Non-Hispanic white
People with disabilities	81	73	71	77	57%
Young adult parishioners	80	72	73	72	60
Immigrants	78	68	66	52	39
Non-English speakers	77	65	62	55	35
Inactive Catholics	76	70	63	70	53
Hispanics, Latino(a)s	76	59	59	54	38
Divorced parishioners	76	65	65	66	54
Low-income families	75	69	67	68	46
Non-Catholic spouses	74	67	66	65	55
New parishioners	72	73	67	68	50
African Americans, Africans	72	61	66	57	39
Asians, Pacific Islanders, Native Hawaiians	71	66	60	57	38
American Indians, Native Alaskans	71	62	62	71	39

Source: Gray 2015b

cultures in the parish community. American Indian or Native Alaskan respondents show slightly higher yet still minority patterns of agreement on these statements.

Respondents were also asked if they agreed that their parish should be more involved in welcoming specific groups (Table 8.4). Generally Hispanic parishioners are more likely than others to "strongly" agree that their parish should be more involved in welcoming members of the groups listed. At the other end of the spectrum, non-Hispanic white parishioners are generally least likely. Regardless of self-identified race and ethnicity, majorities of all respondent subgroups "strongly" agree that their parish should be more involved in welcoming people with disabilities, young adult parishioners, inactive Catholics, divorced parishioners, and non-Catholic spouses.

Half or fewer non-Hispanic white parishioners "strongly" agree that their parish should be more involved in welcoming new parishioners (50 percent), low-income families (46 percent), immigrants (39 percent), African Americans, Africans (39 percent), American Indians or Native Alaskans (39 percent), Hispanics or Latino(a)s (38 percent), Asians, Pacific Islanders, or Native Hawaiians (38 percent), and non-English speakers (35 percent). Note that any group listed that indicated social class, language, race, ethnicity, or immigrant status drew minority "strong" agreement from non-Hispanic white parishioners.

PARTICIPATION IN PARISH ACTIVITIES

Respondents were asked about their interest in participating in parish activities and programs other than attending Mass. As shown in Table 8.5, fewer than four in ten non-Hispanic white parishioners surveyed said they were "very much" interested in anything that was listed. By contrast, half or more of the responding Hispanic parishioners said they were "very much" interested in every program and activity they were asked about.

Hispanic parishioners express the most interest in outreach programs to at-risk youth (73 percent), Catholic volunteer or aid organizations

Table 8.5 Parishioner Interest in Activities

	Percentage Responding "Very Much"				
How Interested Would You Be in the Following?	Hispanic	Asian	Black	American Indian	Non-Hispanic white
Outreach programs to at-risk youth	73	52	65	56	38%
Catholic volunteer/aid organizations	63	53	63	50	35
Language classes for parishioners	62	44	54	42	29
Whole family catechesis classes	60	42	48	49	22
Small faith communities	56	40	46	40	22
Catholic fraternal societies	55	38	48	37	23
Community service or volunteering	54	53	62	48	36
Charismatic renewal	53	41	53	40	19
Efforts to register voters	51	41	58	42	29
Cursillo	50	36	40	29	17

Source: Gray 2015b

(63 percent), and language classes for parishioners (62 percent). Asian and black parishioners also show high levels of interest for outreach programs to at-risk youth (73 percent) and Catholic volunteer or aid organizations (63 percent), along with community service and volunteering (53 percent and 62 percent, respectively).

Many of the programs and activities with the highest levels of interest involve the parish community reaching out to the broader community.

Other than those self-identifying as non-Hispanic white, respondents may be expressing a greater desire for their parish to be active in the local community. Non-Hispanic white parishioners may view parish life as more internally focused and show less interest in outreach to the wider community.

Two questions in the Culturally Diverse Catholic Parishes Study were replicated from the Emerging Models Study in-pew surveys. Comparing the results from the two sets of surveys, non-Hispanic white parishioners in parishes nationally are less likely than those in multicultural parishes to strongly agree that having people of different cultural backgrounds enriches their parish (51 percent compared to 64 percent) and that parishioners of different cultures participate in parish life together (30 percent compared to 37 percent). Thus the pattern of responses for non-Hispanic white parishioners observed here may not be limited to multicultural parishes.

CONCLUSION

As Brett Hoover (2014) has observed, the new reality in culturally diverse parishes is quite different from that experienced by the Catholic immigrants of the 19th and early 20th century, who primarily came from European Catholic countries. In many cases those immigrants were able to establish their own, more homogeneous "national" parish communities. The immigrants of today are coexisting in "shared parishes." Hoover writes, "On the one hand, immigrants and their families find a safe space in which to congregate and worship in their own language in a culturally familiar idiom. They do so without disrupting the worship and ministry groups already in residence" (2). By doing so two or more groups of parishioners are connecting in the same space, sometimes in shared worship and community and at other times avoiding each other. A single parish community does not emerge. Hoover concludes, "The shared parish can easily become kind of a permanent crucible of grief where resentments and frustrations dominate the scene over time. It can be turned into a kind of waiting room that permits immigrant groups to manage their own cultural expressions of religiosity but only until such time as they can be pragmatically coerced into adapting Euro-American religious customs" (222).

Since the end of World War II the percentage of U.S. adults identifying as Catholic has remained a remarkably stable figure at about 25 percent. Yet beneath this stability lies enormous cultural change. Immigration, varying levels of fertility across the population, religious switching, and migration have transformed the demography of the population and the culture of parish life in the United States. This is a process that is likely to continue in the decades ahead. How Catholics in the pews respond to these changes and how pastors and bishops adapt will determine the future of the Catholic parish in America.

The next chapter again uses the in-pew survey of Catholics from the Emerging Models Study to examine the attitudes of these Catholic parishioners about being Catholic and about their experience of parish life. We explore their attitudes about parish life, what attracts them to their parish, and their feelings about the increasing cultural diversity in parish life.

CHAPTER NINE

THE VIEW FROM THE PEWS

What Catholic has not heard complaints of parishes with dull music, boring homilies, poor parishioner participation, or ethnic divisions that prevent parishioners from uniting into a single parish community? Is this the experience of the typical Catholic in the pew?

In fact it is not. CARA's in-pew surveys of parishioners in 23 randomly selected parishes across the United States, conducted in 2012 as part of the Emerging Models Study, found that parishioner evaluations overall tended to be very positive. More than 90 percent of parishioners who were surveyed in their pew during Mass said they are satisfied with their parish. Of course, as we noted in chapter 7, parishioners increasingly are seeking out parishes that best meet their needs and preferences, a phenomenon known as "parish shopping" or "parish hopping." In fact 35 percent of parishioners in this study were attending Mass at a parish of their own choosing rather than their territorial parish, compared to just 14 percent of core Catholics in the Notre Dame Study who admitted this (Gremillion and Castelli 1987: 55). This practice is more common among younger Catholics and among those who identify their race and ethnicity as something other than non-Hispanic white. And instead of saying they go to Mass out of obligation or habit, they are most likely to say they attend because of the importance they place on the Eucharist and the meaning they find there.

PARISH SATISFACTION

Overall 56 percent of parishioners surveyed in pew for the Emerging Models Study rate their satisfaction with their parish as "excellent" (92 percent rate their satisfaction as either "good" or "excellent"). One explanation for this high level of satisfaction with parish life may be that those attending Mass today do so because they find the experience an enjoyable one. They are in the pew because they want to be there, not because they feel morally obliged to attend. While we do not have comparable data for the period prior to Vatican II, today nearly six in ten Catholics nationally agree that "one can be a good Catholic without attending Mass weekly" (Gray and Perl 2008: 61). Such an opinion directly contradicts catechetical sources like the *Baltimore Catechism*, so frequently used in religious education before Vatican II. In fact available data do suggest that U.S. Catholics are not attending Mass with quite the regularity they did in years past. As was mentioned in chapter 7, Polling research from the 1960s estimated that 55 percent of adult Catholics attended Mass weekly in 1965, compared to the 24 percent CARA polls report in 2015 (CARA Frequently Requested Church Statistics). Taken together these data suggest that those attending Mass weekly today are more likely than those fifty years ago to be in the pews because they want to be there and not out of some sense of moral obligation, social pressure, or guilty conscience.

Catholics in pew do not find everything equally satisfying, however. Some areas of parish life are more satisfying (such as worship and faith formation), and some are less satisfying (such as evangelization, outreach, and the sense of community).

BEING CATHOLIC

Compared to adults nationally who choose Catholic when asked on a survey to identify their religion, in-pew Catholics are considerably more likely to identify themselves as proud, practicing Catholics. Fully 98 percent of in-pew Catholics surveyed by CARA either "somewhat" or "strongly" agree they are proud to be Catholic, and 95 percent "somewhat" or "strongly" agree that they are a practicing Catholic. In comparison 77 percent of Catholics nationally at least "somewhat" agree they are proud to be Catholic, and 55 percent at least "somewhat" agree they are a practicing Catholic. The contrast increases when examining those who "strongly" agree. Those in pew are 32 percentage points more likely than Catholics nationally to "strongly" agree they are proud to be Catholic (87 percent compared to 56 percent) and are more than twice as likely to "strongly" agree they are practicing Catholics (69 percent compared to 33 percent).[1] As we see in the Emerging Models Study, these in-pew Catholics find much at their parishes that attract them.

ELEMENTS THAT ATTRACT PARISHIONERS TO THE PARISH

The Emerging Models Study found that the element that most attracts parishioners to a parish is an open and welcoming spirit. Parishioners say they were "very much" attracted to their parish by its open, welcoming spirit (68 percent) and the sense of belonging they feel there (64 percent). Sixty-two percent were attracted by the quality of the preaching, and 60 percent to the quality of the liturgy. Core Catholics from the Notre Dame Study gave similar reasons for attending their particular parish: the quality of pastoral care and concern provided by the parish priests, the qualities of friendliness and/or concern among members of the parish, the style of worship typical of the parish, and the quality of preaching at Mass (Gremillion and Castelli 1987: 55).

Figure 9.1 ranks the various elements of parish life that in-pew parishioners in the Emerging Models Study say attract them "very much." Besides its open, welcoming spirit, the sense of belonging they

1. These comparisons to in-pew Catholics are from CARA's Parish Life Surveys, conducted at hundreds of parishes across the United States since 2000 (CARA 2014b). The comparisons to self-identified Catholics nationally are from CARA's study *Sacraments Today: Belief and Practice among U.S. Catholics* (Gray and Perl 2008).

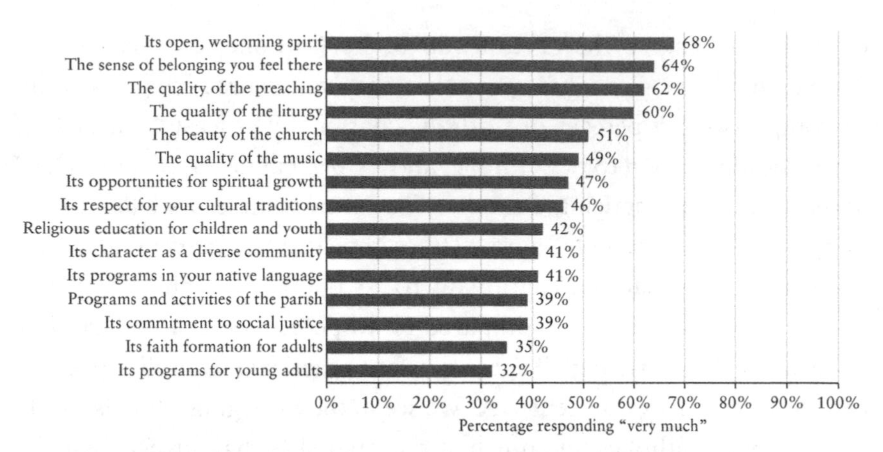

Figure 9.1 Elements That Attract Parishioners to a Parish.

Source: Gray et al. 2013.

feel, and the quality of the preaching and liturgies, about half mention the beauty of the church and the quality of the music. Not coincidentally these are elements parishioners would experience at a weekend Mass.

Parishioners across all races and ethnicities rank their parish's open and welcoming spirit and the sense of belonging they feel there as the top two elements that attract them to their parish. Comparing parishioners across various racial and ethnic categories does expose some differences particular to specific ethnicities:

- Asian or Pacific Islander and Hispanic/Latino(a) parishioners are among the most likely to cite the beauty of their church as something that attracts them "very much." They are also more likely than other groups to be "very much" attracted by the quality of the music, the programs and activities of the parish, its religious education for children and youth, its faith formation for adults, and its opportunities for spiritual growth.
- Black parishioners are more likely than other groups to cite the parish's character as a diverse community as a top attraction. They are among the least likely to say they are "very much" attracted to their parish by its religious education for children and youth.

- White parishioners are among the least likely to cite the beauty of the church, its character as a diverse community, its respect for cultural traditions, or its programs in their native language as aspects that attracted them "very much."

PARISHIONER EVALUATION OF ASPECTS OF PARISH LIFE

As we said, 56 percent of parishioners evaluate their overall satisfaction with the parish as "excellent," with an additional 36 percent rating it as "good." Altogether, then, some 92 percent of those in the pews report a positive experience at their parish.

Parishioners were also asked to evaluate several aspects of parish life, such as worship and sacraments, faith formation, evangelization, hospitality, community, stewardship, and parish leadership. Between 86 and 96 percent report positive experiences with all of these, with the sacramental and worship life of the parish especially likely to receive positive evaluations.

Examining only "excellent" ratings, shown in Figure 9.2, parishioners are particularly likely to highly evaluate their parish's celebrations of the sacraments (67 percent), followed by its hospitality or sense of welcome

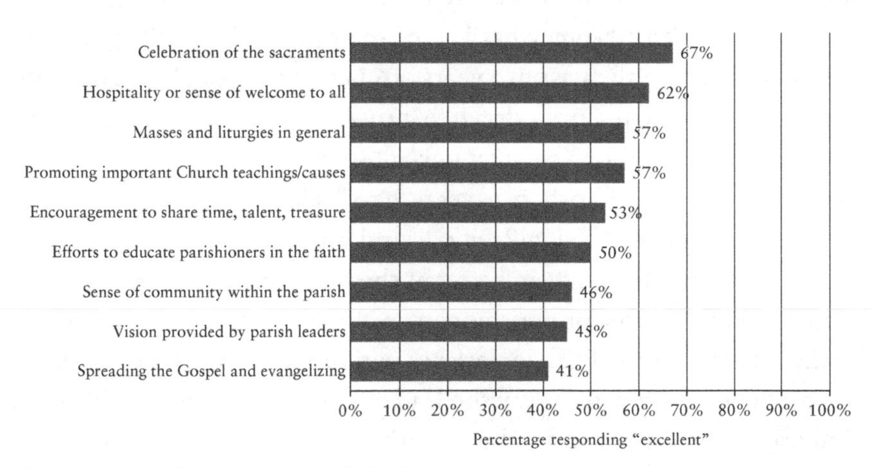

Figure 9.2 Evaluation of Parish Life.

Source: Gray et al. 2013.

to all (62 percent), Masses and liturgies in general (57 percent), and the way the parish promotes important Church teachings and causes, such as protecting life and helping the needy (57 percent). Least likely to receive high ratings are measures of parish life related to evangelization, the vision provided by parish leaders, and the sense of community within the parish; less than half give an "excellent" rating to these three aspects of parish life.

Ethnic groups do not always have the same experience of parish life. Asian/Pacific Islander parishioners (56 percent) are most likely to give an "excellent" rating to parish efforts in spreading the Gospel and evangelizing, for example. Black (31 percent) and white (39 percent) parishioners, on the other hand, are relatively less likely to do so.

PARISH LEADERSHIP AND DIRECTION OF THE PARISH

Despite the turbulence that many parishes have experienced in recent years due to parish mergers and closings in many dioceses of the Northeast and Midwest as well as explosive growth and increasing diversity, particularly in suburban parishes in the South and West, parishioners surveyed in their pews for the Emerging Models Study appear to have weathered these challenges well. They recognize the changes: most (86 percent) at least "somewhat" agree their parish has undergone significant changes in the past five years; 46 percent "strongly" agree with this statement. The majority disagree, however, that these changes have affected parish life. Just 37 percent even "somewhat" agree that "things were better at this parish five years ago." Unlike the other groups, though, 63 percent of Asian/Pacific Islander parishioners agree at least "somewhat" that things were better at the parish five years ago.

Eighty-nine percent of parishioners evaluate the leadership provided by their pastor (or the PLC, in parishes with no resident priest pastor) as at least "good"; 57 percent say the leadership is "excellent" (Table 9.1). Similarly 84 percent evaluate the pastor's vision for the parish as at least "good." White and Asian/Pacific Islander parishioners are more likely

Table 9.1 Parish Leadership

	"Good" or "Excellent"	"Excellent" Only
Leadership provided by the pastor or PLC	89%	57%
Vision provided by the pastor or PLC	84	45
	"Somewhat" or "Strongly Agree"	**"Strongly Agree" Only**
I would feel comfortable talking with the pastor or PLC.	92%	54%
There is sufficient qualified parish staff to meet the parish's needs.	83	34
I feel well informed about parish finances.	82	35
Parish pastoral council members are accessible to me.	81	29
I am comfortable with the idea of sharing staff (such as youth ministers) with neighboring parishes.	87	35

Source: Gray et al. 2013.

than black or Hispanic/Latino(a) parishioners to evaluate the pastor's leadership as "excellent," while Asian/Pacific Islander parishioners are most likely and black parishioners least likely to rate the vision provided by the pastor or PLC as "excellent."

The view from the pews is that pastors are still accessible and approachable. More than 90 percent of parishioners feel comfortable talking with their pastor. Eighty-three percent agree "somewhat" or "strongly" that their parish has sufficient qualified staff to meet the parish's needs. More than 80 percent feel parish pastoral council members are accessible, and the same proportion believe they are well informed about parish finances. Overall it appears that parishioners have adapted to the changes in parish life and still feel comfortable with the structure. As a matter of fact they have adapted to the changes so well that close to 90 percent say they are comfortable sharing parish staff with neighboring parishes, an adaptation that many pastors have employed when they are pastoring more than one parish.

These attitudes are not shared equally by all parishioners, however. For example, black and white parishioners are more likely than Asian/Pacific Islander or Hispanic/Latino(a) parishioners to "strongly" agree they feel comfortable talking with the pastor. At the same time Asians/Pacific Islanders and Hispanics/Latino(a)s are more likely than blacks or whites to "strongly" agree they are comfortable sharing staff with other parishes.

Finally, 61 percent of parishioners agree they have a role in the decision making of the parish; 17 percent "strongly" agree with that statement. Whether or not they are actively involved in the life of the parish, they feel (at least "somewhat") their opinions are being heard. Once again Asian/Pacific Islander parishioners are more likely than other groups to "strongly" agree with this statement.

PRIORITY GIVEN TO ELEMENTS OF PARISH LIFE

The Emerging Models Study asked parishioners to state which areas they feel their parish should prioritize. As presented in Figure 9.3,

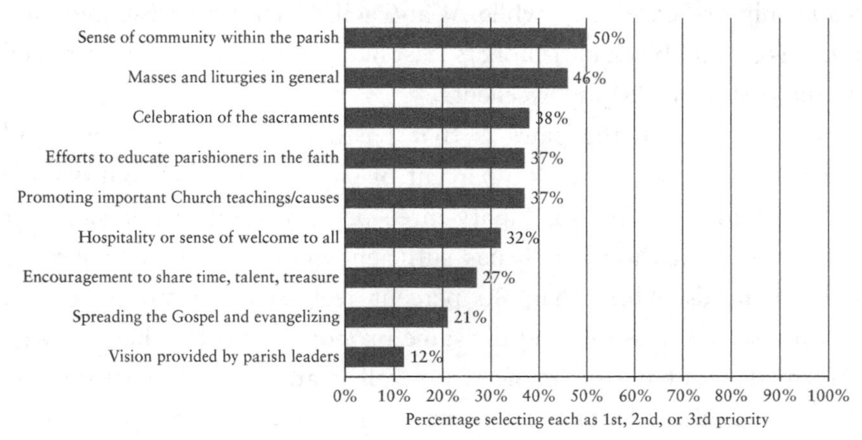

Figure 9.3 Priorities for Parish Life.

Source: Gray et al. 2013.

parishioners are most likely to mention the sense of community within the parish and its Masses and liturgies in general among their top three priorities for parish life. It is interesting to note that the sense of community is among the top three priorities for almost half of parishioners, since about the same proportion rated their parish as "excellent" in that aspect, as we saw in Figure 9.2.

Also notable are the elements least likely to be mentioned among top priorities for parish life: those related to leadership, evangelization, and stewardship. We will see later in this chapter that parishioners also show little enthusiasm for sharing their time and talents with the parish or for evangelization efforts promoted by the parish.

While parishioners of all four generations are equally likely to list the sense of community and the Masses and liturgies in general among their top three priorities, the generations differ on their priorities for some of the other aspects of parish life. Members of the two oldest generations are a little less likely than those of the two youngest generations, for example, to prioritize efforts to educate parishioners in the faith. At the same time parishioners of the youngest generation are a little more likely than the older generations to prioritize hospitality or sense of welcome and spreading the Gospel or evangelizing.

Parishioners of different ethnic backgrounds also express different priorities for parish life:

- Asian/Pacific Islander and Hispanic/Latino(a) parishioners are more likely than others to list promoting Church teachings/causes among their top priorities. In fact among Hispanic/Latino(a) parishioners this aspect has higher priority than promoting a sense of community within the parish.
- Black and Hispanic/Latino(a) parishioners are especially likely to list among their top priorities encouragement to share one's time, talent, and treasure. Black parishioners are also more likely than other groups to list the vision provided by parish leaders among their top three priorities.
- Hispanic/Latino(a) parishioners are more likely than others to identify efforts to educate parishioners in the faith among

their top three priorities. They are relatively less likely to list the sense of community within the parish among their top three priorities.

- White parishioners are more likely than other groups to identify hospitality or sense of welcome and celebration of the sacraments among their top three priorities for parish life.

ATTITUDES ABOUT CULTURAL DIVERSITY

As we saw in chapter 8, cultural diversity within U.S. parishes varies widely; some parishes experience great racial or ethnic diversity, and others very little. Nevertheless, as the diversity of the U.S. Catholic population increases, so too does the diversity within parish life. We examine here some of the views from the pews about this increasing diversity and how it is experienced in parish life. Table 9.2 displays the range of attitudes expressed by parishioners on four statements relating to their experience of diversity in parish life. More than three in four at least "somewhat" agree with each of these statements about cultural

Table 9.2 Attitudes about Cultural Diversity in the Parish

	"Somewhat" or "Strongly Agree"	"Strongly Agree" Only
Having people of different cultural backgrounds here enriches this parish.	95%	55%
I am comfortable with the increasing racial or ethnic diversity of this parish.	93	49
Parishioners of different cultures participate in parish life together.	85	34
The diversity in the parish is reflected in the diversity in the parish staff.	75	29

Source: Gray et al. 2013.

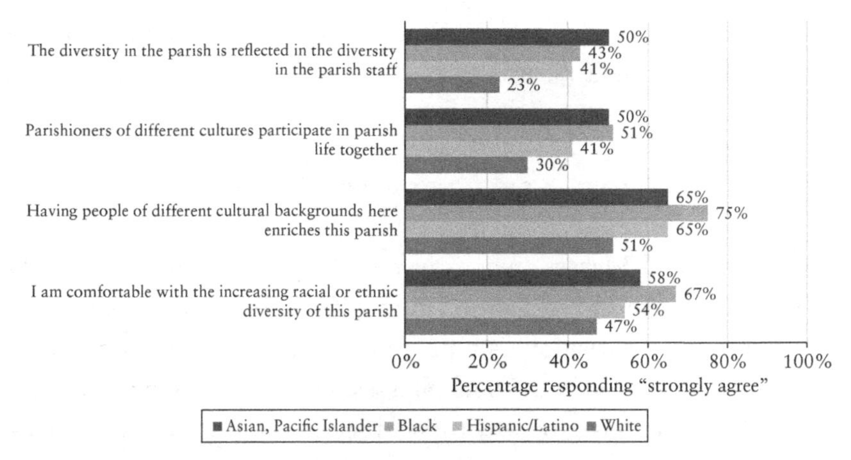

Figure 9.4 Attitudes about Parish Diversity, by Ethnicity.
Source: Gray et al. 2013.

diversity in their parish. Parishioners are especially likely to agree that having people of different cultural backgrounds enriches their parish and that they feel comfortable with the increasing racial or ethnic diversity of their parish.

Examining only those who "strongly" agree with the statements, even greater differences emerge. More than half "strongly" agree that cultural diversity enriches the parish, and half agree as strongly that they are comfortable with the increasing diversity of the parish. A third "strongly" agree that parishioners of different cultures participate in parish life together, and about a third agree as strongly that the diversity in the parish is reflected among its staff.

Generational differences are also apparent here. Members of the youngest generation of parishioners, who have grown up in an increasingly diverse society, are significantly more likely than older generations to "strongly" agree with each of the statements in Table 9.2. At the same time white parishioners, who are more likely to be found in the older generations, are least likely of the various ethnicities to "strongly" agree with any of these statements about cultural diversity (Figure 9.4). Hispanics/Latino(a)s are also a little less likely than black or Asian parishioners to "strongly" agree that parishioners of different cultures participate in parish life together. Black parishioners, on the other hand, are particularly likely to "strongly" agree they are comfortable with the increasing diversity of their parish and that this diversity enriches their parish.

EVALUATION OF ASPECTS OF WORSHIP

Because weekend Masses (where in-pew Catholics responded to the survey) are their most frequent contact with their parish, it is not surprising that these parishioners report high evaluations of many of the areas of worship present at these Masses. Here we also explore some of the reasons they give for why they attend Mass, from CARA's Parish Life surveys (Center for Applied Research in the Apostolate 2014b), conducted in the pews at parishes across the United States since 2000.

With two exceptions, three-quarters of parishioners responding to CARA's Parish Life surveys have had a positive experience of each of the areas of worship evaluated. Those areas of worship receiving "excellent" evaluations from about half or more of parishioners include weekend Masses in general, the greeters, the parish's hospitality or sense of welcome, the weekend Mass schedule, opportunities to worship in one's native language, the liturgical decorations and environment, the homilies, and the music. Notice that the three aspects of parish life that were evaluated by parishioners in the Emerging Models Study—Masses and liturgies in general, hospitality or sense of welcome to all, and celebrations of the sacraments—also received "excellent" evaluations from at least half of parishioners surveyed. In contrast one-third or fewer give "excellent" ratings to their parish's small prayer groups, opportunities for devotions, people's participation in worship, and Confession or Reconciliation.

Although the Notre Dame Study did not ask core Catholics to evaluate their parish experience in quite the same way, we can observe that two-thirds or more of core Catholics from the Notre Dame study rated the music, the readings, the prayers, and the ritual at their parish as "generally satisfactory" (Gremillion and Castelli 1987: 137).[2]

2. The Notre Dame Study used the 3-point scale of "generally unsatisfactory," "could be improved," and "generally satisfactory." It also measured satisfaction

Those responding in pew to CARA's Parish Life surveys were also asked a few questions to understand their reasons for attending Mass. Four of the top seven reasons parishioners give have to do with their positive experience there: the importance of receiving Communion (81 percent say this reason "very much" explains why they attend), the meaning they find at Mass (77 percent), the sense of belonging they experience (72 percent), and the help they get from hearing homilies weekly (63 percent). Fewer say they attend because they want to set an example for their children, they feel obligated to attend, or they attend out of habit. Very few say they attend because it is part of marrying/settling down or for social reasons.

The Notre Dame Study similarly asked core Catholics about their reasons for attending Mass. Although the questions were slightly different and the way they were measured is not directly comparable, we notice the same ordering of reasons for attending Mass: the most cited reason was "I enjoy the feeling of meditating and communicating with God," followed by "I enjoy taking part in the service and experiencing the liturgy." About one in five said they attend because "I feel a need to receive the Sacrament of Holy Communion" or "I feel a need to hear God's Word." One in ten said they attend because they "want to set an example" for their children. Even fewer say they attend out of obligation or out of habit. Very few say they attend for social reasons (Gremillion and Castelli 1987: 132).

EVALUATION OF FAITH FORMATION

As we noted in our discussion of Figure 9.2, half of parishioners say their parish does an "excellent" job in its efforts to educate parishioners in the faith. When asked to evaluate the particular faith formation

with homilies, but rather than ask about their satisfaction with homilies in general, it asked parishioners to rate them on how inspiring, interesting, and informative they are, as well as how much the homilies help them with their faith. Nearly six in ten rated the homilies on the upper part of the scale in terms of how inspiring and interesting they were. Fewer than two in ten gave them a positive rating for how informative they were or how helpful they were with their faith.

Table 9.3 Evaluation of Faith Formation Programs

	"Good" or "Excellent"	"Excellent" Only
Sacramental preparation for		
First Reconciliation and Eucharist	95%	57%
Confirmation	94	56
Baptism	94	55
RCIA (process for becoming a Catholic)	94	53
Marriage	93	52
Other formation/religious education programs		
Children's religious education	90%	52%
Adult faith formation	88	43
Youth ministry	85	46
Bible study	81	38
Small faith sharing groups	80	36
Retreats	77	36

Source: Gray et al. 2013.

programs, they show most enthusiasm for efforts directed at sacramental preparation and faith formation for children and teens. Table 9.3 shows that sacramental preparation programs are among the most highly rated aspects of parish life, with more than half giving them an "excellent" evaluation. Among the other programs evaluated, parishioners are generally more satisfied with parish formation programs that pass on the faith to the next generation than with those involving their participation in small groups or retreat programs.[3]

3. Although the questions were not asked of parishioners in the Emerging Models Study, parishioners in CARA's Parish Life surveys were asked how likely they are to engage in some formation-related behaviors in the next year. Two-thirds seem mostly lukewarm about learning more about their faith in any of the ways asked about; only a third say they are "very" likely to spend time learning more about their faith in the next year; a quarter say they are "very" likely to regularly

Parishioners of different generations had very similar evaluations of each of these faith formation programs. Parishioners of different ethnicities, however, displayed some differences of opinion. In general Asian/Pacific Islander parishioners evaluated each of these programs more highly than did the other ethnic groups, while black parishioners tended to evaluate each of them less favorably. Hispanic/Latino(a) and white parishioners evaluated each program somewhere between the other two groups.

STEWARDSHIP OF TIME, TALENT, AND TREASURE

Figure 9.2 shows that more than half of parishioners surveyed in the pews feel encouraged by their parish to be good stewards, sharing their time, talent, and treasure with others. Sharing of time and talent through volunteer service or becoming more involved in parish ministry appears to be something parishioners recognize as a need but seem to be somewhat reluctant to engage in. They do, however, show more openness to sharing their "treasure" in their willingness to contribute financially to the parish.

About six in ten agree at least "somewhat" with each of the statements about stewardship presented in Table 9.4. Examining only those who "strongly" agree with each statement, about half say they feel invited and encouraged to participate more in parish ministries, and about a third understand how to become more involved in ministry. A fourth report that parish leaders encourage them to explore their vocation within the parish, and almost a third indicate they readily volunteer when help is needed. Only about a fifth, however, "strongly" agree they have an interest in being more involved in parish ministry or feel called to have a greater role.

read the Bible; and a fifth indicate they are "very" likely to participate in a small faith-sharing group.

Table 9.4 Stewardship of Time and Talent in the Parish

	"Somewhat" or "Strongly Agree"	"Strongly Agree" Only
I feel invited and encouraged to participate in parish ministry	91%	47%
It is clear to me how to become more involved in the ministry of my parish	82	32
Parish leaders encourage me to explore my vocation within the parish	78	26
I am interested in being more involved in the ministry of my parish	76	22
I readily volunteer when help is needed	74	29
I have felt a calling to a greater role in parish ministry	59	18

Source: Gray et al. 2013.

Among ethnic groups, we note that Asian/Pacific Islander parishioners are more likely than others to "strongly" agree they have felt a calling to a greater role in parish ministry. They and Hispanic/Latino(a) parishioners are also more likely than others to "strongly" agree they are interested in being more involved in ministry in the parish.

Although the Emerging Models Study did not ask parishioners directly about their financial stewardship, we do have data from CARA's Parish Life surveys that address this topic. These parishioners were asked how likely they are to engage in some stewardship-related behaviors as well as about impediments to increasing their financial contributions to their parish.

When asked about their future stewardship plans, parishioners in these studies appear to be more open to contribute financially to the parish than to give more of their time and talent. Fully 85 percent report being "somewhat" or "very" likely to contribute generously to the support of their parish in the next year; 44 percent report being "very" likely to do so. In comparison 57 percent indicate being at least "somewhat" likely to volunteer for a parish ministry, and 34 percent say they are "very" likely to do so. When asked what prevents them from contributing more financially to the parish, about 25 percent or more say their support of other causes or their current financial status "very much" prevents them from contributing more. Ten percent or fewer say that issues they have with parish spending priorities, the direction of the parish's leadership, or issues with Church teachings "very much" prevent them from giving more financially to the parish.

EVALUATION OF PASTORAL MINISTRY

Overall parishioners seem to be well satisfied with their parish pastoral ministry staff. As seen in Table 9.5, 89 percent of parishioners say the ministry of the professional ministry staff is "good" or "excellent" (48 percent rate it as "excellent"). Similarly 89 percent of parishioners evaluate their parish's director of religious education as "good" or "excellent" (49 percent choose the rating "excellent" only), and 86 percent rate their youth minister as at least "good" (46 percent choose the rating "excellent" only). The parish pastoral council is rated as at least "good" by 87 percent, and 40 percent rate it as "excellent."

Table 9.5 Pastoral Ministry

	"Good" or "Excellent"	"Excellent" Only
Ministry of the pastor or PLC	91%	57%
Director of religious education	89	49
Ministry of the professional ministry staff	89	48
Parish pastoral council	87	43
Youth minister	86	46

Source: Gray et al. 2013.

Parishioners of different ethnicities have somewhat different opinions of the pastoral ministry in their parishes. Asian/Pacific Islander and white parishioners are more likely than black or Hispanic/Latino(a) parishioners to evaluate the ministry of the pastor and of the professional ministry staff as "excellent." Black parishioners are least likely and Asian/Pacific Islander parishioners most likely to evaluate the ministry of the youth minister as "excellent."

EVALUATION OF PARISH OUTREACH

Although parish outreach was not evaluated in the Emerging Models Study, data from the CARA Parish Life surveys suggest that this is the area of parish life least likely to receive positive evaluations. To what extent parishioners see such outreach to groups within the parish (e.g., families) and outside the parish (e.g., inactive Catholics) as the responsibility of parish leaders rather than the individual's own responsibility is less clear.

Comparatively parishioners are more likely to give the parish a high rating for its outreach to some groups than others:

- Parish outreach to visitors and guests (38 percent) is most likely to receive an "excellent" rating, followed by new parishioners (29 percent). Parish outreach to inactive Catholics (19 percent), on the other hand, is seen as very successful by fewer parishioners.
- Parish outreach to those sick or homebound (38 percent) and to those with disabilities (32 percent) is particularly likely to receive an "excellent" evaluation.
- Families and children also fare well. Some 37 percent give an "excellent" rating to parish outreach to families, and 33 percent give a similar rating to outreach to children. Fewer give an "excellent" rating to outreach to married couples (26 percent), widows and widowers (22 percent), those divorced or separated (19 percent), and single adults (17 percent).

- Efforts to reach out to these age groups received an "excellent" rating from a quarter to a third of parishioners: senior citizens (34 percent), adults age 36 to 64 (31 percent), teens (30 percent), and young adults (27 percent).

Parishioners are especially likely to rate their parish as successful at reaching out to families in crisis and those in financial need, with more than 67 percent giving their parish a positive evaluation in these areas. Fewer, about 50 percent, give a positive evaluation to parish outreach to single parents or to those with addictions.

Another way to gauge satisfaction with parish outreach is to examine to what extent parishioners themselves feel included in parish life. Nearly 90 percent at least "somewhat" agree they feel included in parish life, and 49 percent "strongly" agree with the statement.

EVALUATION OF PARISH COMMUNICATIONS

According to CARA's Parish Life surveys, eight in ten parishioners evaluate parish efforts to communicate with parishioners as at least "good." More than eight in ten at least "somewhat" agree they feel well informed about what goes on their parish. Nearly four in ten "strongly" agree they do.

The most effective ways of communicating with these parishioners are still those related to the weekend Masses: 70 percent indicate that Sunday bulletins are "very" effective, and 57 percent say the same about the announcements read at Mass.

CONCLUSION

The view from the pews appears to be quite similar to that revealed in the Notre Dame Study some 30 years ago. Despite tremendous change in the Catholic population, pastoral leadership, and parish life itself, parishioners are still attracted to the parish for many of the same reasons: they feel welcome there, they feel a sense of belonging, and they appreciate the quality of the liturgy and the Word of God they receive there. Despite increasing cultural diversity, the elements that attract parishioners to the parish appear to cross ethnic boundaries.

CHAPTER TEN

SUMMARY AND CONCLUSIONS

The Notre Dame Study was groundbreaking in its attempt to conduct a 360-degree view of contemporary parish life. Its methodology of surveying a large number of Catholics and then focusing in greater depth on three dozen parishes enabled its researchers to achieve a thorough understanding of parish life. The 15 reports that resulted from the project were each unique in their ability to study individual topics in depth.

But much has changed in the past 30 years, both in U.S. society in general and with respect to the U.S. Catholic Church in particular. In many ways parish life today is much different than it was 30 years ago. Catholic parishes have been shaped by five trends that, although already under way at the time of the Notre Dame Study, have accelerated in importance since then. These trends are ongoing and will continue to reshape parish life in the decades ahead. At the same time other changes, which are only beginning to emerge on the horizon, will likewise have a huge effect on Catholic parish life going forward.

What are the trends that have significantly impacted parish life since publication of the Notre Dame Study? What have been their primary impacts?

TRENDS

TREND 1: DECLINING VOCATIONS TO ORDAINED AND NONORDAINED RELIGIOUS LIFE

Although the United States is priest-rich relative to the rest of the world, the number of priests has been declining and the number of Catholics per priest has been increasing. This pattern began in the late 1960s, predating the Notre Dame Study, and has continued unabated. During that same period the decrease among nonordained religious sisters and brothers was even more dramatic. As disappointing as these figures are, they mask another trend: the aging of active clergy and vowed religious. Not only are there fewer of them, but they are much older. This trend has been partially mitigated by the growth in the use of foreign-born priests, which introduces its own set of concerns. There has also been a slight uptick in the number of seminarians.

In fact the only clergy group that is growing is the permanent diaconate, which was reestablished after Vatican II. The permanent diaconate did not exist in 1965. Today there are over 18,000 permanent deacons, and 40 percent of parishes are served by at least one deacon.

TREND 2: CATHOLICS' MIGRATION FROM THE INNER CITY TO THE SUBURBS AND FROM THE NORTHEAST AND MIDWEST TO THE SOUTH AND WEST

As we described in a number of chapters, the early waves of Catholic immigrants tended to settle in the urban Northeast or the rural Midwest. That is where they built their parishes and their schools. But following World War II, as their socioeconomic status improved, they began to migrate to suburban communities. More recently, as employment prospects grew in the South and West, Catholics migrated to those parts of the country, leaving behind the inner-city and rural churches and schools that had been built to serve them.

Again this pattern began before the Notre Dame Study, and it continued and in some ways has accelerated, cutting a wider swath, in the period since that study.

TREND 3: GROWTH IN THE U.S. CATHOLIC POPULATION FUELED BY IMMIGRATION

The U.S. Catholic population has continued to grow in numbers, keeping pace with overall population growth in the United States and holding steady at about a quarter of the U.S. population. A significant component of this growth is the result of immigration, especially of Spanish-speaking Catholics but also of Catholics from areas of the world other than Europe. In fact one in four U.S. Catholics was born outside the United States. The Emerging Models Study found that from 2005 to 2010 the average proportion of Caucasians in parishes decreased by nearly 3 percent, while the number of Asian and Hispanic parishioners increased by 17 percent. As many as one in four U.S. Catholic parishes celebrate their weekend liturgies in more than one language.

TREND 4: THE CONTINUING IMPACT OF VATICAN II

Although most of the reforms of Vatican II were already well under way by the time of the Notre Dame Study, the meaning of "the priesthood of the laity" and "lay ecclesial minister" was still being formulated. In the past 30 years lay involvement as an important component of parish life has grown exponentially, culminating in the 2005 USCCB document *Co-Workers in the Vineyard of the Lord*, which officially recognized the importance of well-formed laity serving in parish ministry roles. Arguably even if there had not been a decline in priestly vocations, the laity's role in parish leadership would have expanded as Catholics lived out their baptismal calling to active participation in the faith, as laid out in the documents of Vatican II.

TREND 5: DECLINING PARTICIPATION IN SACRAMENTS

Weekend Mass attendance had been declining during the period leading up to the Notre Dame Study, but rather than slow down the decline has accelerated. Today weekend Mass attendance rates are only about 60 percent of the 1985 rate documented in the Notre Dame Study.

Participation in other sacraments have also been in decline. Since 1985 the U.S. Catholic population that is connected to a parish has grown by 30 percent, but Catholic marriages are *down* by 57 percent and infant baptisms have *decreased* by 27 percent, according to *The Official Catholic Directory*.

Some of these declining rates can be attributed to the clergy sexual abuse scandal and its mishandling by some in the Church hierarchy. However, as chapter 7 points out, much of the decrease in Mass participation can be explained by differences in generations. Within every ethnic group studied, weekend Mass attendance is lower for members of the millennial generation than it is for both the Vatican II and post–Vatican II generations. One possible contributing factor is the increased ethnic diversity among Catholics of that generation and the resultant difficulty that some ethnic populations have in locating a Mass in their language.

Another factor that contributes to these declines in sacramental participation is the frequently mentioned mismatch between the location of Catholics and their parishes. Especially in rural areas that have experienced parish consolidations, some Catholics must drive long distances to attend weekend Mass. And in the increasingly congested suburban parishes in the South and the West, competition for parking spaces in overcrowded parishes discourages some from attending.

IMPACTS

What have been the impacts of these trends on parish life over the past 30 years?

IMPACT 1: THE NEED TO RECONFIGURE PARISH ORGANIZATIONAL STRUCTURES

As a result of the migration of Catholics to the suburbs and the South and West there exists a serious mismatch between the location of Catholic facilities (primarily churches and schools) and the Catholic population. As a generalization the facilities tend to be located in urban areas in the Northeast and Midwest, while the population is increasingly located elsewhere. Large urban dioceses are faced with the need to subsidize poorly attended inner-city parishes and schools while building facilities in the suburbs. Meanwhile dioceses in the South and West are struggling to build new churches as they try to cope with the explosive Catholic population growth.

The impact of migration has been exacerbated by the decline in vocations to the priesthood. The result is that many dioceses, faced with both a shortage of priests and a mismatch between the location of their parishioners and the location of their parish facilities, have found the need to reconfigure their parish organizational structures. This frequently requires the closing or merging of parishes or adopting some of the innovative parish organizational structures permitted by canon law and described in chapter 4. Whatever the method used, the result is larger and more complex parishes and often disaffected parishioners.

IMPACT 2: INCREASE IN MULTICULTURAL PARISHES

The changing demographics of the U.S. Catholic population described in chapters 2 and 8, especially those related to ethnicity, have presented parishes with a new set of challenges.

At one time Catholic parishes in this country were relatively homogeneous, reflecting the propensity for recent immigrants to settle in enclaves with others of similar ethnic backgrounds. This pattern was reinforced by the creation of "national" (ethnic) parishes and strictly enforced parish boundaries. More than a third of U.S. parishes today serve a particular racial, ethnic, cultural, or linguistic community, with many serving more than one. The data show that in many cases parishioners of different cultural backgrounds, rather than forming a single parish community, coexist in "shared parishes." Parishes are challenged by this reality to make a greater effort to become more welcoming in a way that enables community building among all cultures.

IMPACT 3: A GREATER ROLE FOR LAITY

No longer consigned to "pray, pay, and obey," the laity have found many leadership opportunities in their parishes. The decline in vocations to both the ordained and vowed religious life has opened the door for the laity to carry out the promises of Vatican II. Few parishes could operate today without the professional laity filling roles such as director of religious education, youth minister, music minister, pastoral associate, business manager, and myriad other ministry roles that were once held by clergy, vowed religious, or volunteers. In fact CARA has estimated that there are nearly 40,000 lay ecclesial ministers in parish ministry in the United States today, an increase of more than 80 percent since 1990. Reflecting the increased opportunities for participation as lay ecclesial ministers, there has been a corresponding growth in the number of programs to support the laity and ensure that the Church is served by qualified laity. CARA estimates suggest there are more than 22,000 laity enrolled in a variety of lay ministry formation programs to prepare for future ministry, primarily in parishes.

Lay parishioners are not only making their mark as paid staff. Most parishes support a variety of ministries led by and staffed with volunteers. Canon law recognizes the importance of laity serving on formal parish advisory councils, such as the finance council (mandated by canon law) and the pastoral council (which canon law leaves to the discretion of the diocesan ordinary). As we explained in chapter 4, there are even cases where the laity are asked to lead a parish by serving as a parish life coordinator under canon 517.2.

IMPACT 4: EFFECT ON PARISH AND DIOCESAN FINANCES

A combination of factors has coalesced to place increasing stress on parish and diocesan finances. One is the mismatch between the location of the Catholic population and the location of parish facilities, alluded to frequently in these pages. Many dioceses, particularly in the Northeast and Midwest, are saddled with antiquated facilities, frequently in the inner city, that necessitate large maintenance expenses while serving few Catholics. At the same time these and other dioceses are charged with providing new facilities to serve parishioners who have migrated to the suburbs and into the South and West.

The rapid growth in the number of lay ecclesial ministers, while applauded on a number of levels, has resulted in a similar growth in personnel costs for parishes. While still in some cases undercompensated relative to other areas of work, these lay ecclesial ministers receive many times the compensation formerly paid to clergy and vowed religious, who were expected to serve on a minimal stipend.

One thing that hasn't changed since the time of the Notre Dame Study is that Catholics' financial contributions in support of their parish still lag far behind those of their Protestant friends.

EMERGING TRENDS

These trends and their impacts are not likely to dissipate in the near future. But just as emerging trends at the time of the Notre Dame Study took on added significance over the following 30 years, so too one can expect emerging trends to impact U.S. Catholic parishes over the next 30 years. In their early stages it is typically difficult to identify emerging trends, but one that is clearly visible is the impact of technology.

Parish leaders are only now beginning to understand the role that technology plays in their parishioners' lives and how to adapt to it. By now most parishes have recognized the importance of having a website, although most have not tapped into its full potential. Parishes are grappling with ways to keep up with the latest changes in social media usage. It is clear that millennials value the ability to be connected via social media; their children are likely to be even more dependent. Parishes will need to utilize the current generation of social media and keep up with rapid advances in the way technology enables their parishioners to communicate.

Technology also promises to change the way parishes operate, ranging from advances in parish management software that will allow them to collect detailed data on parishioners in order to better serve them, to the use of electronic transfers of parishioner contributions and parish expenditures. And technology has revolutionized the way Church leaders, notably the Pope, can communicate directly with parishioners on a routine basis.

A FINAL WORD

Parishes in the United States, and in fact the Church in general, have experienced a variety of changes since researchers at Notre Dame conducted their seminal study. The very nature of parish life, which today is dominated by parishes that tend to be organizationally complex and multicultural, is dramatically different than it was in the mid-1980s. The nature of parish leadership has changed. Parishioners' attachment to their parish, including attendance at weekend Mass, has changed.

But many things have not changed, including the centrality of the Eucharist to parish life, the efforts of dedicated clergy and lay people to serve God while serving their parishioners, and the attitude of parishioners who recognize that the Church, as a human organization, will make mistakes, but who remain faithful and committed nevertheless.

There are many reasons to be optimistic about the future of U.S. Catholic parish life over the next 30 years.

APPENDIX

DATA SETS USED

Some of the data and results presented in this volume are from existing CARA research published elsewhere. In some cases other published data, including those from the Notre Dame Study of Catholic Parish Life, are shown or referenced. In these cases that original published source is cited. Most results presented are from several recent CARA surveys and databases. These are described below.

EMERGING MODELS OF PASTORAL LEADERSHIP

In 2009 the Emerging Models of Pastoral Leadership Project, a collaboration of five Catholic national ministerial organizations funded by the Lilly Endowment, commissioned the Center for Applied Research in the Apostolate at Georgetown University to conduct three surveys in parishes nationwide. The first of these was a single-informant survey to develop a portrait of parish life in the United States today. This was followed by surveys of parish leaders in a subsample of these parishes as well as in-pew surveys with their parishioners. The data from these studies are archived at CARA.

PARISH SURVEY

The parish survey is based on a partially stratified random sample of 5,549 U.S. parishes. The stratification of the first 3,500 parishes sampled was based on weighting by the archdiocesan or diocesan averages of the percentage of the Catholic population and the percentage of the number of Catholic parishes in the United States in each archdiocese or diocese as reported in *The Official Catholic Directory*. This stratification ensured that parishes representing the full Catholic population were included rather than a sample dominated by areas where there are many small parishes with comparatively small Catholic populations. CARA also sampled an additional 2,049 parishes using simple random sampling. These parishes were selected to ensure that the survey included at least 800 responses. Following a series of reminders and a field period from March to December 2010, a total of 846 parishes responded to the survey, for a response rate of 15.3 percent. The margin of sampling error for the survey is ±3.3 percentage points.

PARISH LEADER SURVEY

The second survey for the project included responses from 532 parish leaders (e.g., parish staff, finance and pastoral council members, other parish leaders) in 246 of the parishes from the first survey (margin of sampling error of ±4.2 percentage points). This survey was in the field from May 2011 to April 2012. Parish leaders include all staff—ministry and nonministry, paid and volunteer—in the parish as well as all parish finance council members, pastoral council members, and up to 10 other individuals identified by the pastor or parish life coordinator (a deacon or lay person entrusted with the pastoral care of a parish under canon 517.2) "who exhibit leadership in the parish community."

These parish leaders were drawn from a subset of parishes completing the Phase 1 survey as well as in-pew surveys of parishioners for the overall project. Additionally a random sample of 930 parish leaders, identified by their pastors and parish life coordinators from the first phase, were invited to respond. Another 100 pastors and parish life coordinators from the first survey were asked to distribute surveys to all of their parish finance council members. It is not possible to calculate a response rate for this sample as we cannot be certain how many finance council members were given the survey. As an estimate it is likely that no more than 2,500 parish leaders in total were invited to take the survey.

IN-PEW SURVEY

The third survey for the project, summarized in this report, was conducted in parts of 2011 and 2012 and includes 14,437 parishioners surveyed in pew in a subset of 23 parishes randomly selected from the first phase. All parishes were guaranteed anonymity within the project as part of their agreement to participate. Stratified random selection was used to select a sample of 70 parishes to ensure geographic variability and the inclusion of oversamples for Emerging Models–type parishes (i.e., multicultural, PLC, MPM, and consolidated). Additionally five parishes were selected by the partners to represent specific parish types. Thus, in total, 75 parishes were chosen for potential participation in the third phase, and 65 were invited by the time data collection ended. Five refused to participate, and 10 uninvited parishes were held in reserve at the time data collection ceased. Thirty-five percent of the 65 invited parishes (i.e., 23 parishes) participated in the project. Another 35 percent verbally agreed to participate in the third phase of the project but did not follow through with all of the steps required by the time data collection for the study was ended. The most common reasons cited for an inability to participate before the deadline were related to scheduling issues. Many parishes refused to consider or schedule surveys during Lent or Advent, and CARA also faced some resistance for scheduling during summer months. The remaining 14 invited parishes (22 percent of the sample) either did not come to an agreement to participate (without declining) or did not respond with a decision by the cut-off date after repeated invitations to participate.

The framework for the research was loosely based on the Notre Dame Study of Catholic Parish Life, conducted in the 1980s. That research included surveys in 36 parishes. The Notre Dame Study evolved over seven years, whereas the parish research for the Emerging Models Study was completed in two years. The partners instructed CARA to cut off data collection from in-pew surveys in the fall of 2012.

It is not possible to calculate a margin of error for the in-pew surveys as these are not randomly selected Catholic Mass attenders nationally and are instead all Mass-attending, participating adults and teens in the pews at an Emerging Models Study parish on a given Sunday. However, as a rule of thumb consistent with statistical inference using survey data, we use a difference of greater than ±6 percentage points between subgroups to establish an indication of a real difference in the population.

Geographically seven of the parishes were located in the Northeast, three in the Midwest, seven in the South, and six in the West. This distribution is similar to the percentages of the U.S. Catholic population residing in each region within 3 percentage points or less, with the exception of the Midwest, which has 13 percent of the parishes in Phase 3 but 21 percent of the adult Catholic population according to the most recent CARA Catholic Poll (Center for Applied Research in the Apostolate 2012). The average number of in-pew respondents in parishes was 628. The largest parish produced 2,508 respondents and the smallest 68.

EMERGING MODELS BISHOP FOCUS GROUPS

In October 2005 the Emerging Models of Pastoral Leadership Project at the National Association for Lay Ministry commissioned CARA to conduct a series of focus groups with U.S. bishops to explore theological issues related to parish life coordinators in canon 517.2 parishes. CARA conducted six focus groups between October 2006 and April 2007. Each focus group included between five and 12 bishops from a specific province or region. Focus groups lasted an average of 75 minutes. Each group was recorded digitally and later transcribed. Each group was invited to include a theologian of their choice for the purpose of providing clarification where needed. In all, the data include 45 participating bishops.

NATIONAL SURVEY OF CATHOLIC PARISHES

In October 2013 CARA began sending invitations to 6,000 randomly selected parishes (5,000 by email and 1,000 by postal mail) to take part in the National Survey of Catholic Parishes (2014). Stratification was used. The total number of parishes randomly selected in each diocese was determined by weighting the diocesan averages of the percentage of the Catholic population and the percentage of Catholic parishes in the United States in each diocese as reported in *The Official Catholic Directory*. This stratification ensures that parishes representing the full Catholic population were included rather than a sample dominated by areas where there are many small parishes with comparatively small Catholic populations. A total of 486 email addresses were not valid, and 68 of the invitations sent by post were returned as bad addresses or as being closed parishes. Thus the survey likely reached 5,446 parishes. The survey remained in the field as periodic reminders by email and postal mail were made until February 2014. Reminders were halted during Advent, and the survey closed before Lent in 2014. A total of 539 responses to the survey were returned to CARA for a response rate of 10 percent. This number of responses results in a margin of sampling error of ±4.2 percentage points at the 95 percent confidence interval. Respondents include those returning a survey by postal mail or online. Responding parishes match closely the known distribution of parishes by region. Data for sacraments celebrated also match the *The Official Catholic Directory* closely. This survey was made possible through funding provided by SC Ministry Foundation and St. Matthew's Catholic Church in Charlotte, North Carolina.

THE OFFICIAL CATHOLIC DIRECTORY

CARA has compiled a database of statistics published in *The Official Catholic Directory*. First published in 1899 by P. J. Kenedy & Sons, *The Official Catholic Directory* is produced annually. The volume provided information about Church personnel, parishes, and other Catholic institutions by diocese. Dioceses report annual statistics about the number of people providing ministry to the Church, as well as Catholic population, numbers of institutions, and sacramental totals.

CATHOLIC MINISTRY FORMATION DIRECTORY

The *Catholic Ministry Formation Directory* (e.g., Gautier et al. 2015) is the result of an annual data collection conducted by CARA for institutions and enrollments in Catholic ministry formation programs. It is the reference volume for seminary, diaconate, and lay ministry formation programs, vocation offices, career counselors, parishes, and many others. It includes statistics on seminarians, deacon candidates, and men and women preparing for lay ecclesial ministry positions. CARA began collecting enrollment data for priesthood formation programs at the theologate, college, and high school levels in the United States in the 1967–68 academic year and has done this annually since. Since 1994 CARA has counted pretheology students studying at theologates, college seminaries, and other sites in its totals of theology-level seminarians. CARA has been conducting studies of lay ministry formation programs nearly every year since 1994. CARA completed the first study of diaconate formation programs in 1996–97 and has updated the information at the beginning of each academic year since then. Trends in these data are presented in a statistical summary of the *Catholic Ministry Formation Directory* annually.

CARA CATHOLIC POLLS

Since 2000 CARA has conducted more than 25 national surveys of adult Catholics. In some cases samples have been broader, including teenagers, and at other times they have included working-age Catholics, Catholic parents with children in the home, and never-married Catholics. Most often they have studied about 1,000 adult self-identified Catholics in the United States. CARA has always surveyed in English and Spanish. Some of the early polls were conducted by telephone with random sample survey methods (resilient distributed data set). Later surveys were conducted with the Knowledge Panel at Knowledge Networks/GfK Custom Research (i.e., surveys taken on computers, tablets, smartphones, or televisions). This volume includes data from two of these.

SACRAMENTS TODAY

In 2008 CARA began working on a survey of U.S. adult Catholics for the Department of Communications of the U.S. Conference of Catholic Bishops. The focus of the survey is participation in the sacramental life of the Church as well as beliefs about the sacraments. In February 2008 CARA polled 1,007 adult self-identified Catholics via Knowledge Networks. A total of 1,485 randomly selected panel members previously identified as Catholic in the panel were emailed the survey. Responses were received from 1,007 of these individuals, for an intrapanel response rate of 68 percent. This sample size yields a margin of sampling error of ±3.1 percent.

NEW MEDIA USE STUDY

In summer 2012 the USCCB commissioned CARA to conduct a national poll of adult Catholics to measure their use of new media. CARA developed a questionnaire and partnered with GfK Custom Research (formerly Knowledge Networks) to conduct the survey in September 2012. The survey was completed by 1,047 self-identified Catholics who were 18 or older, resulting in a sampling margin of error of ±3.0 percentage points. Sixty-seven percent of the panel members invited to take the survey completed it.

CARA PARISH LIFE SURVEYS

CARA has been conducting in-pew surveys in Catholic parishes since 1994. These studies are for diocesan and parish planning. Those commissioning the surveys choose from a catalog of CARA questions. Thus CARA has survey data from more than 1,000 parishes and more than 375,000 respondents. For this volume CARA has used parish averages from all surveys conducted since 2000. This includes surveys conducted in more than 800 parishes nationwide between 2000 and 2015. These data represent the largest and most comprehensive compilation of surveys conducted in U.S. parishes.

CULTURALLY DIVERSE CATHOLIC PARISHES STUDY

In 2013 the Secretariat for Cultural Diversity in the Church of the USCCB commissioned CARA to estimate the size and distribution of black or African American, Asian American or Pacific Islander, Hispanic or Latino(a), and American Indian or Alaskan Native Catholic populations in the United States, as well as the locations of Catholic parishes known to serve these communities. CARA identified parishes that self-identify as serving or are known to serve racial, ethnic, cultural, and/or linguistic groups in the United States. CARA combined a dozen databases of parish addresses and information, including some provided by the Secretariat. CARA then cleaned the database of duplicates and updated any missing or incorrect information. CARA identified a total of 6,332 parishes that are known to serve a particular racial, ethnic, cultural, and/or linguistic community (35.9 percent of all U.S. parishes). Some of these parishes serve two or three of these communities. Accounting for this, a total of 6,570 communities were identified. In August 2014 CARA began conducting in-pew surveys with parishioners at randomly selected parishes identified by CARA in the first phase of the project (i.e., the 6,332 parishes serving communities) and later recruited to participate in the project. The data used here include the respondents in 27 parish communities that completed the survey as of October 2015. In total 11,044 teens and adults have completed surveys in these communities.

REFERENCES

Bendyna, RSM, Mary E. and Mary L. Gautier. 2009. *Recent Vocations to Religious Life: A Report for the National Religious Vocation Conference.* Washington, DC: Center for Applied Research in the Apostolate.

Benedict XVI. 2009. "Church Membership and Pastoral Co-responsibility." Address of His Holiness Benedict XVI at the opening of the Pastoral Convention of the Diocese of Rome. Basilica of St. Kohn Lateran, May 26. https://w2.vatican.va/content/benedict-xvi/en/speeches/2009/may/documents/hf_ben-xvi_spe_20090526_convegno-diocesi-rm.html.

Center for Applied Research in the Apostolate. 2012. CARA Catholic Poll September 2012. [Data file]. Washington, DC: Center for Applied Research in the Apostolate.

Center for Applied Research in the Apostolate. 2014a. CARA National Survey of Catholic Parishes 2014. [Data file]. Washington, DC: Center for Applied Research in the Apostolate.

Center for Applied Research in the Apostolate. 2014b. CARA Pastoral Assistance Surveys and Services In-Pew Cumulative Statistics 2000–2015. [Data file]. Washington, DC: Center for Applied Research in the Apostolate.

Center for Applied Research in the Apostolate. Frequently Requested Church Statistics. http://cara.georgetown.edu/frequently-requested-church-statistics/.

Conference for Pastoral Planning and Council Development. 2014. "The Role and Reality of Parish Business Managers and Parish Finance Council Members." https://www1.villanova.edu/content/dam/villanova/VSB/publications/2014%20Emerging%20Models%20of%20Pastoral%20Leadership%20Project%20The%20Role%20and%20Reality%20of%20Parish%20Business%20Managers%20and%20Parish%20Finance%20Council%20Members.pdf

Conway, Daniel. 1992. *The Reluctant Steward.* St. Meinrad, IN: St. Meinrad Seminary.

Cooperative Congregational Studies Partnership. 2010. Faith Communities Today Survey 2010. [Data file]. Hartford, CT: Hartford Institute for Religion Research, Hartford Seminary.

D'Antonio, William V., Michele Dillon, and Mary L. Gautier. 2013. *American Catholics in Transition.* Lanham, MD: Rowman & Littlefield.

Davidson, James D., Andrea S. Williams, Richard A. Lamanna, Jan Stenftenagel, Kathleen Maas Weigert, William J. Whalen, and Patricia Wittberg. 1997. *The Search for Common Ground: What Unites and Divides American Catholics.* Huntington, IN: Our Sunday Visitor Press.

DeLambo, David. 2005. *Lay Parish Ministers: A Study of Emerging Leadership.* New York: National Pastoral Life Center.

Froehle, Bryan T., Mary L. Gautier, and Mary E. Bendyna, RSM. 1999. *The Study of the Impact of Fewer Priests on the Pastoral Ministry.* Washington, DC: Center for Applied Research in the Apostolate.

Gautier, Mary L., and C. Joseph O'Hara. 2011. *The Profession Class of 2011: Survey of Women and Men Religious Professing Perpetual Vows.* Washington, DC: Center for Applied Research in the Apostolate.

Gautier, Mary L., Jonathon C. Holland, and M. Connie Neuman, eds. 2015. *Catholic Ministry Formation Directory.* Washington, DC: Center for Applied Research in the Apostolate.

Gautier, Mary L., and Paul Perl. 2000. *National Parish Inventory.* Washington, DC: Center for Applied Research in the Apostolate.

Gautier, Mary L., Paul M. Perl, and Stephen J. Fichter. 2012. *Same Call, Different Men: The Evolution of the Priesthood since Vatican II.* Collegeville, MN: Liturgical Press.

Gautier, Mary L., and Thomas P. Gaunt, SJ. 2015. *A Portrait of the Permanent Diaconate: A Study for the U.S. Conference of Catholic Bishops 2014–2015.* Washington, DC: Center for Applied Research in the Apostolate.

Gautier, Mary L., Tricia C. Bruce, and Mary E. Bendyna, RSM. 2007. *Listening to the Spirit: Bishops and Parish Life Coordinators.* Washington, DC: Center for Applied Research in the Apostolate.

Gautier, Mary L., et al. 2014. *Bridging the Gap: The Opportunities and Challenges of International Priests Ministering in the United States.* Huntington, IN: Our Sunday Visitor Press.

Gray, Mark M. 2012. *Perspectives from Parish Leaders: U.S. Parish Life and Ministry*. Washington, DC: Center for Applied Research in the Apostolate.

Gray, Mark M. 2015a. *Research Review: Lay Ecclesial Ministers in the United States*. Washington, DC: Center for Applied Research in the Apostolate.

Gray, Mark M. 2015b. *Preliminary Topline and Sub-group Report for In-pew Interviews in Culturally Diverse Catholic Parishes*. Washington, DC: Center for Applied Research in the Apostolate.

Gray, Mark M., and Mary L. Gautier. 2012. *Consideration of Priesthood and Religious Life among Never-Married U.S. Catholics*. Washington, DC: Center for Applied Research in the Apostolate.

Gray, Mark M., Mary L. Gautier, and Melissa A. Cidade. 2011. *The Changing Face of U.S. Catholic Parishes*. Washington, DC: Center for Applied Research in the Apostolate.

Gray, Mark M., and Paul M. Perl. 2008. *Sacraments Today: Belief and Practice among U.S. Catholics*. Washington, DC: Center for Applied Research in the Apostolate.

Gray, Mark M., Mary L. Gautier, and Melissa A. Cidade. 2013. *Views from the Pews: Parishioner Evaluations of Parish Life in the United States*. Washington, DC: Center for Applied Research in the Apostlate.

Greeley, Andrew. 1972. *The Catholic Priest in the United States: Sociological Investigations*. Washington, DC: USCC.

Gremillion, Joseph, and David C. Leege. 1987. *Notre Dame Study of Catholic Parish Life, Report No. 15: Post-Vatican II Parish Life in the United States. Review and Preview*. Notre Dame, IN: University of Notre Dame.

Gremillion, Joseph, and Jim Castelli. 1987. *The Emerging Parish: The Notre Dame Study of Catholic Life Since Vatican II*. San Francisco: Harper & Row.

Hoover, Brett. 2014. *The Shared Parish: Latinos, Anglos, and the Future of U.S. Catholicism*. New York: New York University Press.

Leege, David C., and Thomas A. Trozzolo. 1985. *Notre Dame Study of Catholic Parish Life, Report No. 3, Participation in Catholic Parish Life: Religious Rites and Parish Activities in the 1980s*. Notre Dame, IN: University of Notre Dame.

Murnion, Philip J. 1992. *New Parish Ministers: Laity and Religious on Parish Staffs*. New York: National Pastoral Life Center.

Murnion, Philip J., and David DeLambo. 1999. *Parishes and Parish Ministers: A Study of Parish Lay Ministry.* New York: National Pastoral Life Center.

Neal, SSND deNamur, Marie Augusta. 1984. *Catholic Sisters in Transition from the 1960s to the 1980s.* Wilmington, DE: Michael Glazier, Inc.

Perl, Paul, and Mark M. Gray. 2007. "Catholic Schooling and Disaffiliation from Catholicism." *Journal for the Scientific Study of Religion* 46.2: 269–80.

Pew Research Center. 2015a. "America's Changing Religious Landscape." May 12. http://www.pewforum.org/2015/05/12/americas-changing-religious-landscape/.

Pew Research Center. 2015b. "Participation in Catholic Rites and Observances." September 2. http://www.pewforum.org/2015/09/02/chapter-2-participation-in-catholic-rites-and-observances/.

Second Vatican Council. 1965. *Decree on the Apostolate of the Lay People (Apostolicam Actuositatem)*, no. 10. http://www.vatican.va/archive/hist_councils/ii_vatican_council/documents/vat-ii_decree_19651118_apostolicam-actuositatem_en.html.

Smith, Tom W., Peter Marsden, Michael Hout, and Jibum Kim. 2015. General Social Surveys, 1972–2014 [Data file]. Chicago: NORC at the University of Chicago.

Smith, William L. 2004. *Irish Priests in the United States: A Vanishing Subculture.* Lanham, MD: University Press of America.

Sweetser, SJ, Thomas P. 2001. *The Parish as Covenant: A Call to Pastoral Partnership.* Franklin, WI: Sheed and Ward.

The Official Catholic Directory. 1900–2015. Berkeley Heights, NJ: P.J. Kenedy & Sons.

U.S. Bureau of the Census. 2015. International Data Base [Data file]. Washington, DC: U.S. Bureau of the Census.

U.S. Conference of Catholic Bishops. 2005. *Co-Workers in the Vineyard of the Lord.* Washington, DC: USCCB Press.

U.S. Conference of Catholic Bishops, Secretariat of Child and Youth Protection. 2008–2012. International Priests. [Data file]. Washington, DC: USCCB Secretariat of Child and Youth Protection.

West, Robert, and Charles E. Zech. 2008. "Internal Financial Controls in the U.S. Catholic Church." *Journal of Forensic Accounting* 9.1: 129–55.

Zech, Charles E. 2008. *Best Practices in Parish Stewardship*. Huntington, IN: Our Sunday Visitor Press.

Zech, Charles E., Mary L. Gautier, Robert J. Miller, and Mary E. Bendyna. 2010. *Best Practices of Catholic Pastoral and Finance Councils*. Huntington, IN: Our Sunday Visitor Press.

INDEX